£1·00

LIFESTYLES
Fashionstyles

LIFESTYLES

Fashionstyles

SECRETS OF SUCCESSFUL DRESSING

KATHRYN SAMUEL

ORBIS · LONDON

First published in Great Britain 1986 by
Orbis Book Publishing Corporation Ltd.

A BPCC plc company
Greater London House, Hampstead Road,
London NW1

Printed in Italy

ISBN 0 356 12837 7

CONTENTS

INTRODUCTION

Today, dressing well is all about developing a personal style, rather than religiously following fashion. Indeed, the obsessive follower has been labelled a 'fashion victim' by the style-conscious 'eighties − a far greater insult in current terms than being regarded as anti-fashion or just having given up on the battle of looking good. For style, not fashion, has become the watchword of the decade.

The fashion victim swallows seasonal directives whole, wearing each new look without individuality, regardless of whether it suits her or not − mindlessly seduced by all and everything trendy. Victims don't plan their wardrobes: they just veer wildly from one new fad to the next in an expensive hit-and-miss manner. They're the ones who can be heard to cry 'But I haven't a thing to wear', when their cupboards appear to be brimful.

The stylish dresser understands fashion, even loves it, but her approach is selective. She takes her personality, her shape, her colouring and her life into consideration when setting her style. At the beginning they are conscious and deliberate guidelines but they soon become instinctive and confident criteria in selecting all the clothes she buys. From this firm base she goes on to add her own individual and creative touches.

All of us have fallen into the category of victim at some time. Some people feel they never seem to get their clothes quite right. Few belong to the elite band who understand their own style and keep it up to date, which has nothing to do with age and everything to do with attitude. The aim of this book is to help everyone to discover the secret of successful dressing, by keeping fashion in perspective and to find a basis for your own very personal style.

In the first section we go right back to basics. Learn just how important colour can be for clothes and make-up. There are many colours certain people just shouldn't attempt to wear, as they drain rather than flatter various skin and hair colourings. Discover all about proportion, the changes fashion makes to an acceptable silhouette and how you can disguise the figure faults you hate in yourself. Planning a perfect and workable wardrobe to fit the life you lead is not impossible; follow the guidelines and you won't go wrong, from everyday looks to special occasions.

In the second section we take a light-hearted look at style. What is it? Who's to say whether it's good or bad style? What are the vital ingredients of a distinctive style that goes on looking wonderful whatever the dictates of high fashion?

Even if you don't find a character that is a mirror of yourself, you can gain lots of information on the consistency needed to create a style. And after all, there's nothing to stop you being Sloane in the country, Dynasty at night and the archetypal Jet Setter on holiday should you wish. Just as long as you do it with panache − and dare I say it − style.

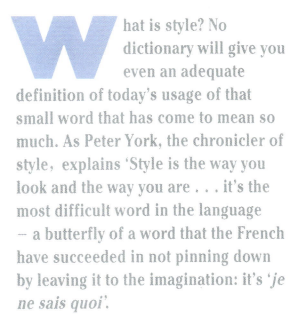

WHAT IS STYLE?

What is style? No dictionary will give you even an adequate definition of today's usage of that small word that has come to mean so much. As Peter York, the chronicler of style, explains 'Style is the way you look and the way you are . . . it's the most difficult word in the language – a butterfly of a word that the French have succeeded in not pinning down by leaving it to the imagination: it's *'je ne sais quoi'*.

Left: In front of photographer Toscani's camera, models hopped, skipped and jumped to make fashion a moving picture show. Here the supremely elegant clothes of Valentino leap into action

Are fashion designers the creators or the interpreters of style? The great ones have undoubtedly been both

Above: Throughout her long working life, Mme Chanel herself demonstrated to perfection the immense wearability of the beautiful clothes she created

To be described as 'a girl with bags of style' is the greatest accolade anyone could wish for. More complimentary than merely being called beautiful, having style implies taste, intelligence, personality. It means looking good, dressing well, being modern rather than fiercely fashionable, presenting through your appearance clear messages of the confident image you have of yourself.

To be deemed 'completely lacking in style' is terrible condemnation indeed. For however much we may hate the superficiality implied by judging by appearances, that is precisely what we all do. To ignore self-presentation as a means of communicating quickly and effectively the positive aspects of your personality is plainly stupid. But then there is a world of difference between someone who dresses to show they have a neat and tidy mind and someone who has that elusive quality, style.

Style as a concept embraces much more in actual fact than just presentation of self in terms of hair, make-up and clothes. For example, your style is carried through to include how you decorate your home, its mood from the walls to the furniture, the knick-knacks you keep rather than discard, the flowers you choose and how you arrange them. Style covers the books you read, the food you cook, the types of exercise you decide to take or the make of car you drive. Overall style includes all these things and more. In this book we are just dealing with dressing with style and mention all those other aspects of life to emphasize the fact that style is something total and needs to be consistent if it is to be convincing.

The stylish dresser first has to decide who she is – or even who she wants to be – before she can pick the look that will reinforce that image. Having said that, it's not often that any of us make such a conscious or calculating decision in the manner of an actress dressing to play a part. More often we are drawn to certain looks in clothes because they coincide with our own personal taste, our character, our lifestyle. The girl with natural style has an instinctive understanding of all these forces and unerringly selects those that suit her.

Many of us, however, have allowed the picture to become blurred by the outside influences of fashion, the way friends we admire look or simply by a lack of direction. It's then you have to go back to basics to learn who you are in order to decide the way you want to look. Discover what your parameters are and then consider your style. Once

you have pinpointed that you are (perhaps!) a red-head with a whimsical nature, a pear-shaped figure, who lives in a flat, works in an office and goes dancing every Friday night, you've made a start. But it's only a beginning. Now you can dip into the enormous style file and pull out a current one that suits, that you feel comfortable with, one you can build on.

For although we like to think of true style as being utterly personal and creative there is a file of acceptable style within which most of us operate. It's ruled by fashion in its broadest sense. Outdated styles get removed from the file, crumpled up and unceremoniously dumped as passé. On-going styles get revamped, others never disappear from one decade to the next, evolving slowly. Sometimes a new file is opened – pretty thin to begin with – which gradually gets fatter as more people adopt the look. Every file gets regularly sifted, the old items being replaced by the newly exciting.

We all have access to the file – but who supplies the information and who decides whether that information is file-worthy? That is the great fascination of style and the most difficult of questions to answer.

Are fashion designers the creators or the interpreters of style? The great ones have undoubtedly been both. Many like to consider themselves artists but their work, however creative, is not comparable to that of a painter who can beaver away in his studio attic, painting to please not prostitute his art. The designer has restrictions – a body, for one – and the necessity of creating and interpreting a style that his customers want to wear *now*.

Coco Chanel once boasted 'I have led fashion for a quarter of a century, because I have been able to give expression to my own time.' Chanel's style and influence is just as strong today and her boast can now be extended to half a century. Chanel understood and recognized the need for the women of her time to be liberated from the stiff, elaborate and rule-bound clothes that were their lot. Women's role was changing, the social order was changing. Chanel's clothes gave expression to those needs with her easy jersey knit suits that were comfortable as well as chic. She began to blur the great divide between men's and women's clothes by suggesting that trousers were not only practical for active busy women but that they could be feminine too. She ridiculed the distinction between the 'haves' and 'have nots' by adorning her clothes with a profusion of quite obviously costume jewellery.

Left: Inès de la Fressange, house model at Chanel, in a black-and-white hound's-tooth check suit (of course) designed by Karl Lagerfeld in 1986. While all the signs of Chanel are there, from the choice of fabric to the important buttons, necktie, rakish hat, and bold jewellery, the look is exactly right for now: narrow body-line, exaggerated shoulders, sleeves casually pushed up, worn with characteristic insouciance

LIFESTYLES FASHIONSTYLES

Above: Great designers have always had the freedom to take fashion to extremes, to make us see things in a new way and even, as witnessed by Lagerfeld's shimmering taps, to make extravagant jokes

All the memorable landmarks in fashion design have reflected or anticipated social demand. The designer who goes down in history is not always the one who does it first but the one who gets it right. Timing is of the essence. Christian Dior's New Look made women feel glamorous and female again after years of uniform and war rationing. A retrograde step maybe, with constricting 18-inch waists, full skirts and high heels, but it was a style that fulfilled a need and was instantly copied world-wide.

In the 'sixties and the early 'seventies everyone was busy breaking all the rules of behaviour and dress. Mary Quant's mini (though many would argue with that claim to possession) was the last moment of fashion dictatorship. Worn by all regardless of status, age or shape, it was (rather like jeans) the great social leveller. You may not remember but if you look back to old photographs even the Queen's skirts rose well above the knee. After the mini nothing was ever the same. A new approach, a new catch phrase entered our fashion language. 'Anything goes' was the slogan, and it spoke volumes. You could be who you wanted to be, act any part, assume the trappings of any culture, dig deep into the dressing-up box and expect your style of dress to be accepted virtually anywhere.

This was 'style' in its iconoclastic heyday since when we've been busily rebuilding a few guidelines, if not rules. Designers like Yves Saint Laurent and Jean Muir have lived through the 'sixties and steadfastedly created clothes for modern woman. Y.S.L., recognizing the extrovert glamour-orientated woman, stuck to his tenets, designing and immortalizing classics (the blazer, the tunic shirt and Le Smoking evening style) that add up to a look which is a lynchpin of the 'eighties. Muir has catered for the woman who prefers a more restrained approach to life. Her line is at once understated, fluid but prim. It is a style that rejects all vulgarity: you may be aware of the body underneath the soft, revealing jerseys, but you will always presume it has taste . . . class and a demure sense of womanhood.

Kenzo Takada headed the Japanese movement to re-think shape and cut. He spear-headed the flat kimono cut in Western fashion, the interest of combining different textures and the jolly jigsaw of a mix of opposing yet compatible prints and patterns. Further developed by Rei Kawakubo, Issey Miyake and Yohji Yamamoto into the popularly labelled 'bag lady' look, the Japanese re-aligned the silhouette, giving us clothes that were even more comfort and wear-orientated than Chanel could ever have envisaged.

Digging up tradition and fuelling our need for continuity was Laura Ashley, and her more rigidly style-oriented counterpoint, American designer Ralph Lauren, telling us that Victorian/Edwardian/Old Money values and dress were worth preserving.

Norma Kamali began the move to the body beautiful with broad (padded) shouldered woman, the fit and healthy exercise Amazon becoming an ideal on which Azzedine Alaïa and Donna Karan built their sexy, motivated career woman image.

Then there's been Katherine Hamnett, whose clothes speak for a group of women whose confident, feminist approach to dress underlined their concern with the wider issues of environment, pollution and world peace. Why spend time ironing when the fabric is intended to be crumpled? Make your point by adopting a universal uniform, unisex some might say, that endorses your opinion as a person, not primarily that of a woman.

Fashion designers put image and viewpoints into clothes. We recognize them, we align ourselves, we decide what we will wear, understanding that this image will communicate volumes about how we see ourselves and how we are.

But in between the designer and the public there is a world of communication, active both before the clothes ever become reality and then afterwards through the choice of the buyers and the way the clothes are displayed in-store and through the fashion magazines.

Street fashion is a phrase endlessly used to describe a style that is evolved on the street, by ordinary mortals. They have no pretensions to being a 'designer' or having any connection with the fashion business world − but they influence them nonetheless. More often than not it is a social clique that sets its own style with far reaching ramifications. The punk movement was perhaps the most dramatic example. Their shock value, their spikey day-glo coloured hair, ripped and torn clothes were soon espoused and thereby anaesthetized by the designers.

WHAT IS STYLE?

Fashion designers put image and viewpoints into clothes. We recognize them, we align our-selves, we decide what we will wear

Above: The new beatnik, cool, knowing, clever, brought streamlined into the 'eighties with Azzedine Alaïa's body-hugging, confident clothes

Right: The girl with the faraway eyes is the one who loves the country look exemplified by Laura Ashley and Ralph Lauren

Below: The classic dresser, always true to a fashion when excellence outweighs the ephemeral, as in the clothes of Jean Muir

Right: Paparazzi wherever she goes. But the Princess of Wales takes obvious delight in the clothes that are a fount of inspiration to the fashion industry

Above: Raunchy, reckless, self-consciously shocking, Madonna launched a look that gave thousands of fashion-hungry pop fans a new identity

It's often a personality that epitomizes a 'street-look' and gives a label to a style

On another tack, delight in the Princess of Wales' style, her photogenic white collars, her carefully co-ordinated formal outfits topped by the obligatory hat and her glamorous evening dresses have given a fillip to a more studied and smart approach from designers.

It's often a personality that epitomizes a 'street look' and give a label to a style. Sometimes it's a film or T.V. soap opera which allows you to identify with the character as well as her visual presentation. Are you at heart an Alexis or a Krystle (*Dynasty*), a Sue Ellen or a Pam (*Dallas*) or a superstar Madonna? Are you an Ungaro-clad Anouk Aimée (*Un Homme et Une Femme 2*) or even a Karen Blixen/Meryl Streep (*Out of Africa*)? The images are endless, their influences small or great depending on current fashionable stance.

Designers show their collections, from the grandest, most up-market to the most accessibly priced mass-market, twice a year. In October they present their ideas for the following spring/summer, in March for the next winter. The shop and store buyers then select the clothes they will stock for the following season and in between the magazines are busy choosing, styling and photographing the looks and the mood of fashion they believe in.

It's through magazines and newspapers that current style, in all its many and varied aspects, is captured in a visual way. There are magazines to cover every conceivable market, age group and taste level, who set out to inform and satisfy their readership with the news, the looks and the moods of current fashion and style.

Magazines with their fashion editors, photographers and models are the image-makers. They interpret the looks of the designers and street influences into readable visual sense. Occasionally the fashion editors who select the clothes go beyond the realms of being reporters of style to becoming adaptors or creators of style in their own right. Diana Vreeland, legendary editor of American *Vogue*, is one who has earned herself an immortal slot in the file of style, with her unerring sense of taste and confidence to make the boldest, brashest of statements with witty accessorizing. Her own uncomprising look, severely bobbed black hair, strong almost ugly features that she accentuates, make her a perfect example of the stylist. Like her, the stylist is often an extremist, providing a strong taste of inspiration that is then watered down for public consumption.

Above: Paloma Picasso, never out of the best-dressed lists and often in clothes by Yves St Laurent, personifies a look that is faultlessly presented yet vibrant and dramatic

Top: Diana Vreeland, renowned editor of American Vogue*, whose personal style defies imitation, with Yves St Laurent, who has had a profound influence on the clothes modern women wear*

LIFESTYLES **F**ASHIONSTYLES

An important question to ask in the search for personal style is 'Do my clothes fit the life I lead?' Are they appropriate to your particular job, whether it is an up-front image-conscious one or a behind-the-scenes organizer? What is perfect for a snappy sales executive may be quite wrong for someone involved in the 'caring' or advice-giving professions. What is practical for a mother who remains at home during child-rearing years may prove too casual a way of dressing at the time when she puts herself back in the job market.

Dressing for work is only one area of your life. You also have to have clothes that suit your social life, both the formal occasions and the relaxed, informal moments. Weddings, parties, beach holidays, days in the country, specialist sports or general exercise, are all events that crop up during the course of a year for most of us. We all need to have the clothes that fill each particular bill to allow us to get on and enjoy the event itself, confident in the knowledge that we're looking good.

Age comes into the equation, but only marginally. Nowadays there are very few looks or styles that can't be worn equally well by a girl of twenty and a woman of forty-five. The way they

Five different lifestyles, each with their own freedoms and restrictions. Do any match yours?

Are you in your early twenties, working hard but having fun? Are you dressing your best in clothes that will help you to go places both career-wise and socially?

Perhaps you are a young mother at home with small children – are you dressing practically while still looking good? How do you deal with jammy hugs on decent clothes?

Have you recently left school and are now in a position to decide how you want to look for a first job or a student's life? How are you going to budget the available funds while discovering your own style?

accessorize them may be different, their choice of fabric or colour may vary from the surprising to the subdued, but otherwise age is no reason for an inhibited approach to dress.

Whether your budget is large or small doesn't make a great deal of difference, as a successful wardrobe relies more on good planning than limitless funds. A huge clothes budget never guaranteed anyone a place on the 'best dressed' lists and sometimes too many things to choose from can mean that no outfit ever gets properly finished off, resulting in a hotch-potch look.

But if you spend time planning your wardrobe at the outset you will save many hours of agonizing that you don't have anything, or at least not enough, of the right things to wear. Try thinking of your clothes as a soap opera. There are the main characters that hold the story together, the everyday clothes that put in an appearance every week without fail. Then there are the minor characters, whose roles may be small but none the less vital – the shirts, sweaters and accessories of your wardrobe. And then there are the guest appearances, the surprise items that give everything else an occasional lift. It's all a question of balance.

Does your varied life call for snappy presentation but leave little time for fuss about clothes? Have you recognized the value of getting together a high-quality basic wardrobe?

Are you re-launching yourself on the job market or revamping yourself for a more sophisticated image? Do you know where to start planning your faultless collection of clothes?

You'll discover detailed wardrobe plans for these five broadly based life-styles on pages 40-61. But don't skip the pages in between: they will help you to choose the right colours and the best shapes for you and will explain the theories behind the basic wardrobe.

There's no doubt that your hair colour and skin tone dictate the colours you can or cannot wear. The wrong shade gives a dull look to skin, eyes and hair, but find the right colours and you'll lift your natural assets on to a higher plane and make them come alive.

ACK TO BASICS

Above: Coolly electric – blue for blondes is classic styling, but you can afford to go for a vibrant shade. Plan your make-up to give subtle emphasis.

Fair- or dark-skinned, brunette or redhead – paint your individual colour scheme boldly across your choices of clothes and make-up.

There's a reason why red will always get you noticed. It's called the 'speed factor'. The eye registers colour at different speeds. Orange takes top position, red holds second place followed by blue, black, green and yellow. Grey is the slowest of all. All-over red is eye-catching but team it with brown and a dash of yellow for a less blinding colour combination.

Right: Brunettes can make the most of mixing pattern and print in strong, contrasting colours. Here a yellow and blue textured sweater tops a multi-coloured flower print skirt for strong impact.

Far right: In granny's era they said 'blue and green should never be seen', but that's just another old colour rule to overthrow. A true blue tweedy jacket and acid green lacy skirt are linked by a green and blue plaid shirt, two of the shades that bring life to a brunette's hair and skin.

t makes no difference whether your hair is mid-brown, dark brown or jet black; whether your complexion is pale, rosy or olive: the range of colours that will suit and flatter every type of brunette is, surprisingly, exactly the same. Of course, you'll have your own preferences – how boring it would be if all brunettes wore nothing but red – but if you want colour to work for you, stick within your spectrum. The range of colours that suits you is very varied and has the advantage of including shades that are always available in the shops.

Learn to judge whether a colour is cool or warm, that is, whether it has a blue or a yellow base. Peachy pink, for example, is a warm, yellow-based colour, while shocking pink is a cool, blue-based one. All brunettes should wear the cool colours, those clear vivid shades that create sharp contrasts.

You'll look your best in true and primary colours – clear red, bright blue, navy, burgundy, turquoise, emerald, pine green, bright lemon yellow, purple and fuchsia. If you like pastel colours keep them icy and clear rather than powdery and muted. Black and strong bright white are also good for you. Avoid the warm golden colours, or the muted, dull shades. Chances are you've already discovered through trial and error that beige and almost every shade of brown flatter you not one jot – although very dark brown (virtually black) can be successful, especially if teamed with a 'fast' primary. (See pages 86-87 for your make-up shades.)

That blondes look good in blue is an unarguable fact of life. All shades from the palest powders to the deepest periwinkles will flatter the fair, delicate tones of your hair and skin, and bring a clarity and sparkle to grey or blue eyes. Combining lots of different blends of blue together, as in this wool jacket, can give a more subtle approach than an outfit in just one shade. Carry it through to green for an added dimension.

Right: Delicate flower print shirt in your best pastels echoes the sky blue waistcoat and pink sunray skirt.

Far right: Soft blue grey coat mixes beautifully with pale pink and muted lavender, knit and tweed.

Soft and cool, pastel and powdery are the colour moods that every natural blonde should remember when choosing clothes or make-up. Your extremely delicate hair and skin tone will not survive an onslaught of brash primaries or heavy dark colours. Bottle blondes, those with golden complexions and anyone who was fair-haired in childhood but is now a gentle brown can stretch the boundaries of the colour range to darker or more vibrant hues; but basically all light-haired, fair-skinned girls should stick with the pale, cool shades.

It's only blondes who look good in beige, especially when it has a rosy pink overtone. Brown is out, but grey from light blue dove shades to charcoal looks marvellous. Blondes may get bored with hearing that pale blue and pink suit them best of all – but there's no getting away from it. Most blues do work wonders, except harsh royal blue, and any navy that doesn't have a lighter greyish tinge. Pinks can go from baby soft to raspberry, but not as far as fuchsia.

All the pastels with bluish undertones, such as light lemon yellow, lavender, eau-de-nil and aqua, are good news. Bright white and stark black, however, are not 'better on a blonde'. There is one notable exception: you *can* wear black at night, as long as you strengthen the colours of your make-up and keep it looking bright. (See pages 84-85 for your make-up shades.)

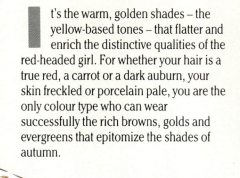

t's the warm, golden shades – the yellow-based tones – that flatter and enrich the distinctive qualities of the red-headed girl. For whether your hair is a true red, a carrot or a dark auburn, your skin freckled or porcelain pale, you are the only colour type who can wear successfully the rich browns, golds and evergreens that epitomize the shades of autumn.

A redhead on a clothes spree should search out these warm colours, steadfastly avoiding any with a bluish tinge. Out with icy or powdery pastels. Steer clear of bright white and black, grey and navy – they're too cold for you, as are the blue-pinks or the blue-reds. In fact blue of any hue is seldom a good colour for the Titian-haired girl. Strong kingfisher or warm, deep turquoise are just about acceptable but as

Browns, golds and greens are a redhead's best colours – mix them all together and you have outfits that are stunning yet subtle.

a general rule treat blue with caution.

All shades of brown, however, from camel to rust, from mahogany to tan will compliment your skin and bring extra lustre to your hair. Just hold a shirt, sweater or dress in any of those hues to your face and watch it come instantly to life. Rich yellow and gold, and all the greens from dark earthy shades to bright emerald or light larch have the same effect. There are few pale colours that look good on the redhead, but cream, oyster, peachy pinks, apricots and rosy beiges are exceptions. Orange and brick reds can look stunning but need to be worn flamboyantly and with confidence. (See pages 88-89 for your make-up shades.)

Colour matching clothes to hair is a smart, effective trick for a redhead to play. Don't try to minimize the eye-catching qualities of your crowning glory – go all out to capitalize on it.

Whether their skin tone is a deep blue black, golden chocolate or light coffee, all dark-skinned girls should keep to very much the same colour palette as a fair-skinned brunette. Muted or murky shades are not for them. It's the brilliant, cool, clear colours that look best.

Ice pastels, sharp yellows, greens and blues – all the blue-based colours – look marvellous on a dark-skinned girl. The same goes for the strong primaries and the hot shades of shocking pink, turquoise and emerald.

If your skin tone is very dark treat equally dark colours with care.

A monochromatic mix of browns can look elegantly chic on a girl whose skin tone is golden. Skin that has blue rather than yellow tones should avoid brown.

Cobalt blue and emerald green make a dashing twosome, playing for effect on plain and patterned fabrics, checks and prints.

Black, charcoal grey, bottle green and mahogany won't highlight your skin or hair because they don't offer enough contrast. White has the reverse effect, but also tends to create too great a contrast.

As a rule the more golden your skin tone and the more red lights you have in your hair, the warmer your colours can be. This group can often wear beige and rich browns well.

All dark-skinned girls take on a coolly elegant look in monochromatic clothes – a mix of light and dark [ ]es of one colour. [ ]t or blue greys work [ ]ades of purple or [ ]d that, a clash of [ ]rs like orange and red, [ ]een can look [ ]if you've got the (See pages 90-91 for [ ].)

Wear strong colours boldly. Here a brash clash of raspberry red and tangerine orange for a jacket, sweater and knit ski-pants combine the two colours with the highest speed factor. Brilliant intense colours and vibrant prints look great on dark-skinned girls.

LIFESTYLES

HEIGHT ....

SHOULDERS ....
(should be approx 1 in (2.5cm)
wider than hips)

ARMPIT ....

WAIST ....
(should be equidistant from
armhole and crotch)

HIPS ....

CROTCH ....
(should be equidistant from height
and ground mark)

*Tall girls can play all kinds
of visual tricks to minimize
their height. The basic plan
is to break the long lean line
and draw the eye
downwards.*

GROUND ....

Developing your own successful personal style depends on the happy marriage of three different elements. Choosing an overall look to suit your personality and lifestyle is essential. Picking colours that make the most of your hair and skin tones is clever. But finally it's the proportions of the clothes you buy, whether they give you a balanced appearance, minimizing figure faults to highlight figure strengths, that will make or break your stylish image.

What is a well-proportioned body? Most of us think of it in terms of bust, waist and hip measurements – the familiar old 34-24-36 syndrome – but these isolated measurements don't necessarily mean perfect proportions. It's your height and build that are the key factors in deciding whether your body is a well-balanced shape.

A good way of discovering whether your proportions are roughly ideal is to strip off and stand bare-foot in front of a full-length mirror. Arm yourself with an old lipstick to use as a crayon. Now make a mark for your height, shoulder bone, armpit, waist, hips and crotch. Your crotch should be equidistant from your height mark and the ground. Your shoulders should be approximately 1 inch (2.5 cm) wider than your hips. Your waist should fall halfway between your armpit and your crotch.

You can also measure your arm; if your elbow marks the middle and is also parallel to your waist your proportions are perfect. The same applies to legs – your knee should mark the centre point.

If all these proportions tally then you know you are the proud possessor of a well-proportioned body – even if that body could do with losing or gaining a few extra pounds in weight. But if they don't match up then you can pinpoint in a positive way where your proportional problems lie and can choose clothes that will minimize rather than accentuate the fact. You'll find specific ideas on how to achieve this on pages 30-33.

Your main bugbear, however, may be that you wish you were several inches taller or not quite so lofty. While there's little either type can do radically to change what nature intended, there are lots of ways to trick the eye of the beholder into hardly noticing the fact.

As an overall plan the short girl should wear clothes that produce a slim vertical shape and an unbroken line. Slim rather than full styles will elongate her body. A one-colour dress rather than separates in contrasting colours will work in the same way. The tall girl who wishes to lose height will achieve it by doing the reverse.

The bean-pole can shorten her stature by wearing big, bold prints and horizontal stripes, the small girl needs tiny prints and vertical stripes. Fabric textures also make a difference – smooth and flat help to keep the unbroken line; knubbly, chunky materials break it up.

If you're small, big accessories, especially outsize shoulder bags and broad brimmed hats, only serve to drag the eye downwards. Wide jacket lapels, shoulder epaulettes and large patch pockets play the same visual trick, making them ideal weapons for the tall girl.

Keeping your accessories positioned high up and your hairstyle small and neat, your shoes and tights in the same colour tone will all help to add height. Contrasting legs and feet, details at the hem of a skirt and a full big head of hair will all give a shortening effect.

But if your body is well-proportioned you may enjoy being tall or petite and not wish to resort to any of this sartorial subterfuge. When it's not you will achieve a more balanced outline if you bear these rules in mind, remembering too that excess weight only serves to emphasize extremes or deficiencies in height. Rules, rules: they're made to be broken – but it's easier to make a stylish rebellion if you know what the guidelines are.

.... HEIGHT

.... SHOULDERS

.... ELBOW
(should be halfway between shoulder and wrist)

.... LEG BREAK

.... KNEE
(should be halfway between leg break and ground mark)

Tiny girls can look short and plump so easily but optical illusions can slim and heighten the frame. Choose clothes that create an unbroken vertical line to draw the eye up to a small neat head.

.... GROUND

29

LIFESTYLES

Eye-deceiving tricks are useful games to play when you are trying to balance the proportions of your body. To play to win you have to understand how the eye reacts to colours and lines. All colours have a 'speed factor'. Orange, red and then blue are the colours that the eye registers the most quickly, followed by green, yellow and finally soft shades of grey. Wear a speedy colour to attract the eye to your good points. For example, wear a red belt on a trim waist or bright blue shoes to highlight smashing legs. Remember too that light colours 'advance' and dark colours 'retreat'. By making use of this fact you can make wide hips less noticeable by wearing a dark skirt and a slim and shapely top half more visible by wearing a light tone.

In terms of line, the eye moves quickly over a vertical but more slowly along a horizontal one. The eye will move rapidly from head to toe when observing a woman wearing a slim dress in one colour. But wear, say, a vivid blue jacket with a black skirt and the eye will linger momentarily where the two colours meet – and if this happens to be your worst or widest point, you are not doing yourself a favour.

Line and colour factors provide the greatest help to the two most common proportional problems, that of the top-heavy girl and the pear-shaped girl. Victoria Principal, whom I once interviewed for *The Mail on Sunday*, regards her generous bust as something she had to 'learn to cope with'. Her solutions to balancing her top half with considerably narrower hips apply to everyone with the same proportional problem. You may consider yours much greater – but I assure you the same rules apply! Everything she wears is based on a V-shape, exemplified by the Dynasty look on pages 104-113. Start with broad shoulders (use shoulder pads if necessary) and let the line skim the bust and gently taper to the knee. Avoid short cropped jackets, high-waisted dresses, broad belts and all bold prints. To balance a large bust the idea is not to make your hips just as wide but to minimize your bosom and keep the silhouette slim.

A good bra is vital: many women make the mistake of not choosing a wide enough cup size, opting for a 36A when a 34C might well give them a more natural line.

Funnily enough, the V-silhouette also works wonders for the pear-shaped girl. But here the idea is to broaden the shoulders in order to make the hips looks smaller by comparison, or simply well-balanced. Padded shoulders or shoulder details like epaulettes, broad sailor collars and full or puff sleeves will all achieve this effect, while halter necks or tight skimpy tops quite obviously will not.

You may be doing everything you can to keep your shoulder line broad and square but make sure you're doing precisely the opposite for your hips and bottom. If the pear-shaped fate is yours you want to avoid bulky or gathered skirts and trousers just as much as any that are too tight. Stick with a slim softly tailored line for skirts or trousers. Remember to make any horizontal line created by a jacket, sweater or tunic top strike well above or below hip level.

Right: Dressing from top to toe in one single colour is not only slimming but also adds height. This dress shape is a good one for anyone with a large bust, with broad shoulders and a dropped arm-hole allowing the dress to skim over the bust to taper gently towards the hemline.

Right: If yours is the pear-shaped figure problem take care to avoid your jacket finishing at your widest point. Choose a strong shoulder line to balance broad hips and pick trousers that are loosely pleated at the waist. Tight trousers or skirts emphasize width and plumpness.

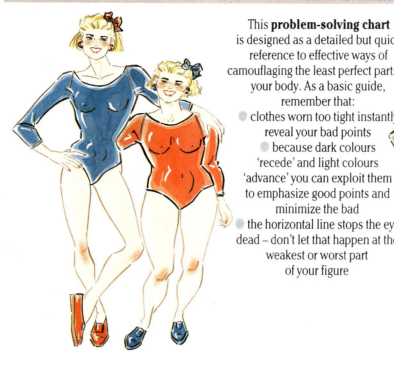

This **problem-solving chart** is designed as a detailed but quick reference to effective ways of camouflaging the least perfect parts of your body. As a basic guide, remember that:

⬤ clothes worn too tight instantly reveal your bad points

⬤ because dark colours 'recede' and light colours 'advance' you can exploit them to emphasize good points and minimize the bad

⬤ the horizontal line stops the eye dead – don't let that happen at the weakest or worst part of your figure

Fault	Avoid	Solutions
Round Face	Any neckline or hairstyle that mirrors the shape of your face. Out go round necklines; jaw length, full hairstyles; high necklines polos or cowls; big round earrings.	In come geometric haircuts; slim face-framing styles; V-necks; revers or open collars; drop or tiny stud earrings.
Square Face	Any neckline or hairstyle that mirrors the shape of your face. Out go square necks; geometric, jaw-length hair; broad earrings.	In comes curly or straight shoulder-length hair; wispy or fluffy short hair; V or scoop necks; revers or open collars; drop or small earrings.
Long Face	Any neckline or hairstyle that mirrors the shape of your face. Out go V-necks, deep open collars; long, straight hair; short, cropped hair; long, drop earrings.	In come round necklines; high necks, polos or cowls; jaw-length hair with body or curl; big broad earrings.
Short Neck	Long hair, straight or curly. Any high collar or choker necklace.	Any short haircut will elongate your neck. Wear open collars, revers or low necklines.
Thick Neck	Short hair, round scoop necklines and chunky chokers.	Longer, soft styled hair; high necklines, mandarins, polos; narrow, deep necklines with collar flipped up; long beads, and scarves.
Long Neck	Very short hair, low necks and long beads.	Elegant necks hardly need camouflage, but long, full hair, high necks, scarves, chokers and broad earrings will do the trick, if you wish.

Fault	Avoid	Solutions
Broad Shoulders	Slash or broad square necklines. Halter neck tops; outsize shoulder pads; shoulder details like epaulettes; puff sleeves.	Raglan, batwing or kimono sleeves; deep or narrow V necks; long beads and scarves.
Narrow or Sloping Shoulders	Raglan, batwing or kimono sleeves. Halter neck tops; narrow, deep V-necks.	Slash or square necklines; puff sleeves, sailor collars; padded shoulders; epaulettes; upward pointing lapels; gathered inset sleeves.
Long Arms	Slim fitting sleeves; any sleeve marginally too short.	Short boxy sleeves; long sleeves with wide cuffs.
Short Arms	Deep cuffs.	Three-quarter sleeves; or roll sleeves up.
Big Bust	High necks; gathers around bustline; high-waisted dresses, skirts or trousers; sleeves ending on a parallel line with bust; horizontal stripes; bloused tops; short jackets.	Open collars and lower necklines; broad shouldered tops; drop waists; semi-tailored, figure skimming clothes; thin belts same colour as top.
Small Bust	Deep cleavage necklines.	Slash necklines; horizontal stripe tops; layer dressing.
Short-waisted	High-waisted styles; broad belts; skimpy, short sweaters.	Drop waists and hip focus clothes; narrow belts same colour as top.
Long-waisted	Narrow belts; drop waist dresses.	Wide belts same colour as bottom half; high-waisted, smock or yoked dresses.
Narrow Hips	Why worry! If you do, avoid slim skirts; tight trousers; skirts with a centre seam.	Baggy, or pleat-top trousers; full, pleated skirts; cropped, boxy jackets.
Broad Hips	Full skirts, pleated or gathered; baggy trousers; patch pockets on hips; wide panel seams on a skirt; jackets that end at hip level.	Softly tailored slim line skirts; same goes for trousers; nothing too tight or too full; below hip level jackets and gilets; button-thru or centre seamed skirts.
Big Bottom	All trousers; full, gathered skirts; fitted jackets.	Softly tailored skirts and jackets; pleated skirts on a broad slim hip basque; long blouson jackets over slim skirt; eye-catching tights and shoes if you have good legs.
Heavy Thighs	Stretch trousers or slim knit skirts; tailored trousers or skirts; SHORT shorts and pedal-pushers.	Dirndl, pleated or gathered skirts; pleat top or straight leg trousers; baggy Bermuda shorts or culottes.
Short Legs	Trousers with turn-ups or gathered ankles; extra long-line jackets; mid-calf skirts; flat pumps; ultra high stilettos.	Separates based on one colour; short jackets; high-waisted dresses; shoes and tights same colour; mid- to high-heeled shoes.
Large Legs	Short skirts; light coloured tights and shoes.	Mid-calf skirts; trousers; dark tights and shoes.

LIFESTYLES

Soft and warm or sturdily protective – winter fabrics are the great comforters. It's hard to think of winter clothes without first imagining their textures; the fleecy feel of sheepskin, the hairiness of the rough tweeds; the fluffiness of woolly sweaters, the toughness of leather and the softness of velvet and fur, all of them superbly tactile and at their aesthetic best in pure and natural fabrics.

Synthetic materials have their advantages, of course: easy to care for, easy to wash, crease-resistant, and always improving. But it's the natural fabrics that have the edge, with their inviting feel and strength or subtlety of colour. They hang or drape with more fluidity, and age gracefully by softening up and fading in tone. Sometimes a small percentage of man-made fibre added to a natural one can produce a fabric which has many of the benefits of each and none of their shortcomings.

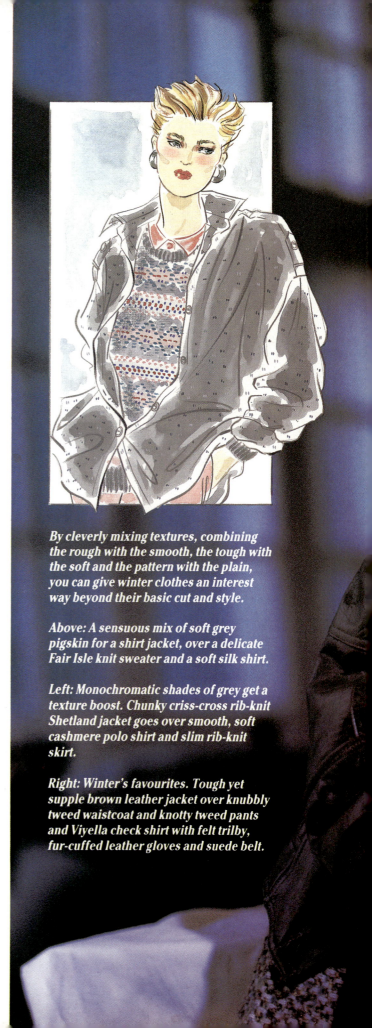

By cleverly mixing textures, combining the rough with the smooth, the tough with the soft and the pattern with the plain, you can give winter clothes an interest way beyond their basic cut and style.

Above: A sensuous mix of soft grey pigskin for a shirt jacket, over a delicate Fair Isle knit sweater and a soft silk shirt.

Left: Monochromatic shades of grey get a texture boost. Chunky criss-cross rib-knit Shetland jacket goes over smooth, soft cashmere polo shirt and slim rib-knit skirt.

Right: Winter's favourites. Tough yet supple brown leather jacket over knubbly tweed waistcoat and knotty tweed pants and Viyella check shirt with felt trilby, fur-cuffed leather gloves and suede belt.

Master of the art of mixing print with print is designer Kenzo, who here manages to combine four different prints in complete harmony. Co-ordinated colour is the key.

BACK TO BASICS

Spots and checks always mix well. Apricot and cream spotted shirt teams with an apricot based madras check skirt.

Not so long ago, mixing two different prints was considered the height of bad taste. How things have changed! Now, far from being deplored, it's clever to mix prints and patterns. Super stylish dressers can break all the rules, mixing four or five different prints, clashing colours and allowing several bold patterns to vie for attention. The less confident mixer can play safe, choosing two prints that share the same base colour. For example, a predominantly kingfisher blue flower print skirt can be teamed happily with a check shirt where the same blue is the major colour. For it's colour rather than the line or design of a print which dictates whether two, three or even four patterns will work together.

It's true that some patterns look better together than others. Spots and stripes always look good, as do checks and stripes. A bold print often combines well with a smaller version; a large flowery fabric will co-ordinate with a tiny floral one; small dots work with large spots; small geometric prints sit comfortably beside larger ones, and broad stripes look at home with thin stripes.

Mixing prints always produces a strong eye-catching outfit, sometimes with an ethnic flavour. Even if an overall palette of prints is too strong a style for you, try adding perhaps a scarf in a pattern different from that of a skirt or trousers for interest and individuality.

Why is cotton summer's predominant fabric? Because its qualities make it simply unbeatable. Economic and easy to produce, its greatest appeal for most pockets is that it's cheap. As a natural fibre it allows the body wearing it to breathe freely unlike synthetic copy-cats. What's more, it's a perfect sponge for dyes of all depths or subtleties resulting in fresh clear colours and prints. Never boring, cotton can be woven or knitted into a seemingly endless range of textures from the finest muslin to the toughest sailcloth, from light cotton jersey to chunky cotton knit sweaters, from universally loved denim to textured picque or seersucker.

For smarter occasions silk is another summer favourite and has many of the qualities of cotton – even the traditionally high price tag on silk seems to get lower year by year.

In spite of valiant attempts by fashion designers to make crumples and creases acceptable and trendy most women feel better dressed without them. This is when a percentage of synthetic fibres can iron out the problem. A ten per cent dollop of polyester helps to prevent creases appearing in a pure linen suit or shirt, which otherwise will only look good for the first five minutes of its first outing. To a lesser extent this also applies to cotton and silk.

Not all summer's materials are smooth in texture. Here a knubbly slub linen suit makes a successful marriage with a white cotton knit sweater, accessorized with chunky beads.

Cotton and silk are summer's favourite fabrics. Here the lightest, brightest white cotton voile over-shirt is worn over a clear blue printed silk tube top and white cotton jersey trousers – three different fabric weights that add more interest to an outfit than the same weight fabric ever could.

WORKING WARDROBES

The perfect wardrobe need be no more than a small collection of clothes, all designed to work together in endlessly versatile combinations. You can start the day looking good and move towards midnight with equal confidence, whether your time is planned to the minute or unexpected invitations arrive.

Above: The simple stylishness of a skirt and loose jacket responds to your mood. Satin in a discreet colour choice is sleekly subtle by day but lights up at night.

Smart to choose the crisp contrast of dark navy and white; smarter still to add the softening touch of warm red in accessories for an informally elegant effect.

Right: **The fundamental jersey coat is a simple style and shape that will work over everything in this wardrobe of clothes. It's worn here with the basic white shirt and navy gabardine trousers. The accessories, a burgundy print wool scarf, a wine leather belt plus blue brooch and earrings, are used to add colour and texture.**

Below: **Raspberry red wool crepe dress is given a daytime look by adding a navy leather belt and topping it with the navy coat.**

The thinking behind a good wardrobe plan applies to every woman's lifestyle whether she is a mother, busy with home and family, a school leaver in search of a job or an established high-powered executive. The degree of smartness or formality you choose for your clothes style obviously has to suit you and the job you do, but the planning approach is the same for everyone. We all have to dress and we'd like to do it well.

There is one vital key to the perfect wardrobe and that is colour. If you start with one basic colour and make sure that you have all the important ingredients in that shade – like a coat or jacket, a good pair of trousers, a simple skirt, a couple of sweaters and essential accessories such as a bag and shoes – you will have laid a solid foundation on which you can gradually build a collection of clothes that suit you perfectly.

When you choose that colour pick one that is literally a basic like black or navy, brown or grey. This wardrobe plan is a long-term strategy, not a short-lived fad, and you need to be certain that your base colour will never be out of style nor out of the shops. In this way it will be easy to make additions to your wardrobe over a period of years.

Once you've chosen that colour, stick with it for all your major buys. It would of course be pretty dull to wear nothing but an unremitting stream of black or grey, but when you branch away from your base colour make sure you always pick a shade that will work well with it.

After colour comes quality. In this plan your clothes are going to be working for you for a long time. They need to last and to stay looking good. If you buy fewer clothes of better quality the chances are that they will.

After quality comes classic. Avoid the fashion gimmicks with your expensive buys and stick to simple, classic, well-cut clothes. Classic does not mean dull or old-fashioned; but, for example, when faced with the choice between a simple wool double-breasted jacket and another with contrasting tartan lapels, pick the former. Don't be frightened by fashion – go for a good strong shoulder line and longer length skirts – but steer clear of fussy trimmings or a very exaggerated cut.

Up-to-date accessories can often bring a much more stylish look than any amount of trendy clothes. So liven up your classics with the accessories of the moment. Try bright contrast colour tights or a large stick pin brooch, use bold scarves or bold earrings to give your outfit a wittier touch.

The pictures on pages 40-45 show a basic wardrobe which provides endless daytime options and also covers every evening function you're likely to attend short of the full-blown ball. There are twelve individual items of clothing giving more than thirty-six different possibilities of combining them.

Navy slub suit has a jacket with a shawl collar, is double-breasted and has a broad shoulder line. The skirt is slim with low-slung box pleats. Here the suit is worn with the navy and beige fine stripe sweater and classic pearls.

Suits can be split and worn separately if the amount of wear is relatively even for each piece. Here the navy jacket works with the burgundy lambswool skirt and sweater over the basic white shirt.

Long and lean, the burgundy skirt and V-neck sweater can be accessorized up or down for day or night. Here it is given a daytime look with the printed wool scarf and pin and worn over the basic white shirt.

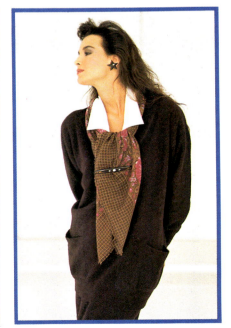

LIFESTYLES

Navy is the base colour with raspberry red and olive green added to liven up the looks, especially for evening. Here are the components for a basic wardrobe.

COAT (1)
Navy jersey in a loose easy shape, roomy enough to go over all jackets. Mid-calf length to work over trousers and all skirt lengths

TROUSERS (1)
Classic navy gabardine with softly pleated top and gently tapered legs

SUIT (2)
Navy slub double-breasted jacket and pleated skirt. Both parts can be worn separately

SHIRT (1)
Vital white shirt in either silk or polyester satin

SWEATER (1)
Navy wool sweater with classic round neck and long sleeves, with a fine beige stripe

DRESS (1)
Raspberry wool crepe dress can be accessorized to work for both day and evening

KNITTED TWO PIECE (2)
Aubergine wool sweater and skirt, both long and lean, both can be used separately

SILK THREE PIECE (3)
Olive satin jacket, green silk pleated skirt and maroon satin vest make a glamorous evening ensemble. Split up and used with daytime separates they make less formal outfits

ACCESSORIES
Flat navy loafers
Navy mid-heeled shoes
Navy shoulder bag
Scarves
Jewellery

Left: The satin separates suit most occasions that require dressing up and (top) mixed with the burgundy skirt cover more relaxed evening outings or smarter daytime appearances.

Above: The green pleated silk skirt brings movement to the burgundy sweater and navy suit jacket.

Right: The raspberry wool crepe dress, worn with a simple string of beads, becomes a convincing after-six style.

LIFESTYLES

CHECKLIST ■ **BASIC JACKET** RE[D] ... **TOP AND SKIRT** BLUE COTTON SWEAT-SHIRTING

You're finished with school. Uniforms and strictly school clothes can probably be consigned to the dustbin for all you care. Whether you are seeking a job or furthering your education, now you have the exciting opportunity to wear what *you* want, to find your own style and learn how to express your personality through the clothes you choose.

Remember that the way you present yourself in clothes, hair and make-up, gives away vital clues about you. Look a mess, and potential employers or tutors might presume that your mind is in the same unco-ordinated condition.

Don't let a small budget stop you from dressing well and in tune with fashion. Just be a little cleverer. Keep up to date by looking at the fashion pages in magazines; watch the changes in shop windows; experiment by trying on lots of styles in shops before you actually buy. Consider the colours that suit you and the shapes that make the most of your height and figure.

First choose your colours. Pick two that work together. In the sample wardrobe on these pages, basic clothes like a jacket, dress, trousers, shirt and sweater are in red and black.

Here is the basic jacket in your compact wardrobe of clothes. Better than a coat, it will work well with all skirts, trousers and dresses. Worn this time with the blue sweatshirt top and skinny skirt, topped with a big wrap scarf, tailed with paisley tights and flat shoes.

Right: The basic jacket meets the basic dress. Long-sleeved black dress in cotton sweatshirting fabric belted in red makes a good interview outfit but won't break the budget.

Short or long, a well-cut head of hair gives you and your clothes extra polish and style.

DRESS BLACK COTTON SWEAT-SHIRTING **TROUSERS SUIT** BLACK & WHITE TWEED

Left: Red and black jacket over red ski-pants, white sweatshirt and red blouse for a casual look. The jacket works with the black dress – the ski-pants with the basic jacket (see previous page).

Right: Black and white check suit looks smart with the red sweater or they can be worn separately.

TROUSERS RED JERSEY PANTS **EXTRA JACKET** RED & BLACK FLECK TWEED **SWEATER** RED SHETLAND **SHIRT** RED COTTON

To the basic red and black we've added a few extras in white or blue to lighten the look occasionally.

By being quite firm about your colour choice you can stretch a few clothes into lots of different combinations. Small budgets become less frustrating with this kind of solid base to your clothes as each month you can confidently build up your collection just by adding a small but useful piece.

Go for jackets rather than coats as they're much more versatile in coping with varying lengths of skirts and trousers. Wind a big, bright scarf around your neck for extra warmth or a splash of colour.

Now's the time when you can wear short skirts teamed with colourful or patterned tights, if you like them and your legs deserve the exposure. The same goes for skinny, stretch ski pants worn with a tweed masculine style jacket or big sweater.

Quality fabric is the major cost ingredient and the first one to suffer in the production of cheaper clothes. In winter, especially when fabrics have to be heavier and warmer, be clever and choose materials like brushed cottons or thick sweat-shirting jerseys that feel good and look more expensive than they are.

SWEAT SHIRT PLAIN WHITE **ACCESSORIES** PAISLEY-PATTERNED TIGHTS, SHOULDER BAG, BELT, FLAT PATENT SHOES, SCARVES

LIFESTYLES

When you are in your early twenties, single if not fancy-free you're probably exploring the possibilities your job has to offer and leading a varied social life. You may well have reached conclusions about the styles and colours that suit you, while still having a great deal of fun with fashion changes.

I hope so anyway. Because you are in a uniquely free period of your life with youth entirely on your side. You can wear the kind of zany clothes you won't get away with in ten years' time. You probably have more time and money to spend on clothes than you ever will have again – later on other responsibilities have a horrible habit of eating up leisure and cash. So make the most of now. Experiment and discover how to make the most of yourself. Learn how to assess a situation and dress to suit it. Master the art of dressing in an individual and stylish way.

Dressing for work is the one area where you may have to exercise a little restraint, projecting through your clothes, make-up and hair an image that will help you to do the job well. The style that is needed for a girl who is front-line reception in an advertising agency is a much more flamboyant, fashion-conscious one than a behind-the-scenes filing clerk in an oil company. If both are ambitious, however, they have a common link. Both need to present an attractively smart image and need a well-co-ordinated wardrobe that underlines their intention of going places.

Only you can assess the right degree of formality for your particular job. Trousers may be fine in one office but too laid-back in another. An executive-style suit may be appropriate for a legal secretary but too off-puttingly officious in a travel agency. As a generalization, co-ordinated separates solve everyone's problem.

It's back to the advice given in the basic wardrobe section at the beginning of this chapter. Make sure that all your basic clothes are in one or two colours that work together. When you buy a sweater or a shirt in another shade, make sure it works with the basics.

This tight working wardrobe plan is based on two colours. Rusty red is the predominant shade, softened by elephant grey. There are two jackets, one a warm, all-weather padded cotton style that is smart enough to wear for work but also casual enough to wear at weekends. The other, a grey jersey blazer, can be teamed with the grey skirt to form a suit or worn with the trousers for a well co-ordinated but more relaxed look. If your job discourages trousers substitute another skirt to the plan.

The padded rust cotton jacket makes a warm and weatherproof topping for working weekdays and weekends away and can be worn with equal ease over the skirt, the trousers and the dress. Add a jaunty beret and cosy gloves for extra warmth.

Inset picture: Striped sweater and check wool trousers combine the two basic colours of rust and grey in a casual yet smart way, dull gold bangles and hoop earrings providing a gleaming finishing touch.

CHECKLIST ■ **JACKET** PADDED RUST COTTON **SKIRT** GREY JERSEY **TROUSERS** RUST/GREY CHECK **DRESS** BUTTON-THROUGH

SHIRT STYLE RUST & ORANGE **SWEATER** RUST & GREY STRIPE **BLAZER** GREY JERSEY **SHIRTS** 1 WHITE WITH RUST STRIPE, 1 WHITE

LIFESTYLES

The button-through shirt dress is a versatile addition to any working wardrobe. It looks good worn as a straightforward dress, either belted or loose. Bright, matching tights give it a more youthful air Or you can wear it as a long jacket over the trousers or the skirt with any of the shirts or sweaters. With any tightly co-ordinated collection of clothes, accessories play a vital role in warding off boredom, so make the most of scarves, ties and jewellery to vary the mood.

Unbuttoned, the shirt dress is worn as a long line jacket over the check trousers and the striped shirt.

Grey jersey blazer forms a suit with the grey skirt and is given high style with a tweedy knit waistcoat, silk tie and pocket handkerchief.

Right: Rust and orange check shirt-style dress looks snappy over toning wool tights.

ACCESSORIES BERET, KNITTED GLOVES, TIGHTS, GREY SUEDE SHOES, SHOULDER BAG, TIE, SILK SQUARE, EARRINGS, BANGLES

LIFESTYLES

Few mothers would reject a jammy hug from a toddler. Or refuse a comforting cuddle to a muddy little monster who had fallen flat on his face in a flowerbed, just because it might mess up their clothes. And that really speaks volumes on the approach mothers of young children have to the way they dress.

It is absolutely no good wearing things that cannot be speedily dumped in the washing machine. It's hopeless if your everyday clothes are uncomfortably smart or too constricting to plonk yourself happily down on the floor to finish the jig-saw puzzle or just to accomplish the less romantic everyday chores.

On the other hand, who wants to look drab or out-of-date? Worse still, to look as if they are so disorganized they don't have time to look after themselves?

To solve all these questions it's best to divide your wardrobe into two halves. One for clothes you can leap into quickly at the beginning of a day and the other for clothes that, although unfussy, are marginally smarter to restore pride in yourself. The two may marry at times when, for example, a smashing sweater livens up your favourite jeans. But on the whole, treat them separately.

For your child-resistant clothes the fabrics you choose are important. Denim is the great stand-by: it looks good, washes well and works in both summer and winter. Corduroy, velours and sweat-shirting fabrics also have these qualities plus the fact that they are not hugely expensive. Cost is, after all, an important factor. Money is possibly tighter now than at any other time of your life and there always seem to be many more vital items to be bought than clothes for yourself. Resist the call to martyrdom – you deserve a few new things each year too!

Choose your colours carefully. With little time to spend on make-up or hair you need colours that do as much as possible for your natural skin and hair tones rather than drain colour from your face (see chapter one). Spanning from palest blue to deepest navy, there's a shade of denim to flatter every type. In style, go for jeans, roomy skirts and the wonderfully comfortable, far-from-dowdy and eminently practical jumpsuit.

CHECKLIST ■ **CHILD-RESISTANT** ■ **JUMPSUIT** DARK BLUE COTTON OR DENIM **JACKET** PALE BLUE DENIM BLOUSON SHAPE

Red double wool cape provides a bright link between casual child-resistant clothes and those, like this blue cable knit sweater and navy gabardine trousers, which give you an instantly smarter look.

Inset picture: Toddler-proof clothes don't have to be sloppy – just practical, easily washable and comfortable. Here the denim blouson jacket with full denim skirt and red sweater proves the point.

SKIRT PALE BLUE DENIM **SHIRTS** 2 COTTON STRIPED SHIRTS **SWEATER** RED CREW-NECK **ACCESSORIES**

TROUSERS NAVY GABARDINE **DRESS** NAVY ROLL-NECK SWEATER DRESS **CAPE** RED DOUBLE WOOL

Left: A jumpsuit makes the perfect uniform for any busy young mother. Snappily fashionable, keeps you tucked in and tidy all day, as neat as a baby in a stretchsuit.

The smarter side of your wardrobe needs a well-cut pair of trousers or a good skirt, whichever suits you better, plus a few soft sweaters and silky-feel shirts. Add a sweater dress or knitted top and skirt that you can accessorize up or down for day or evening, with bright tights and shoes, audacious earrings and big brooches, a good belt or scarf. A coat that will successfully cover the different elements in your dual-purpose wardrobe will be very hard to find so play safe and stick to a jacket or, better still, a swirling cape in a lively colour.

A navy wool sweater dress can be accessorized to take you out in the evening or for smarter daytime functions.

Above left: The denim jacket tops the classically cut gabardine trousers and a bright tartan shirt.

57

■ **SWEATER** BLUE CABLE-STITCH COTTON KNIT **ACCESSORIES** RED BELT & GLOVES, MID-HEELED SHOES, FUN JUNK JEWELLERY

58

CHECKLIST ■ **COAT** GREY MAC WITH WARM CHECK TWEED LINING **JACKET** GREY WOOL TWEED CHECKED IN BEIGE AND CREAM

'**W**omen planning to go back to work after years spent bringing up children don't need clothes – they need confidence.' Those were the immortal words of a doctor friend of mine – which just goes to show how patchy psychological knowledge is in the medical profession.

True, lack of confidence is a bugbear which afflicts most women in that position, who feel that any previous skills they had are pretty rusty and underestimate the organizational skills they have perfected in home-bound years. But what about the confidence to be gained by knowing that you look good, that you're well-dressed in an up-to-date way, looking attractive and making the most of yourself? A good make-up lesson, a sharp hair-cut and new clothes are the easiest way to give yourself a large morale boost.

Using all the advice in chapter one about colour and dressing to solve figure problems, plus the basic wardrobe section at the beginning of this chapter, set out to revamp the old you.

Invest your money – and don't feel guilty about it – in quality rather than quantity. Choose a small collection of clothes that are tightly co-ordinated, that swap around easily and work really well with each other to give you a choice of looks. Get the style balance right by picking a look that is neither too fuddy duddy nor too youthfully trendy.

Smart and formal, the check jacket and the grey skirt meet to make a suit, an important brooch at the neckline providing a gleaming focal point.

Looking relaxed, as the chunky cardigan over an easy polo neck sweater tops the grey flannel trousers.

This grey mac with its warm tweed lining checked in grey, beige and cream forms the core of this wardrobe plan. It will double as a coat, and its generous trench-coat shape gives a casual but stylish look. Teamed here with the slim grey skirt, the look is lightened by the bright cream cable sweater and long scarf.

59

SKIRTS 1 BEIGE PLEATED WORSTED, 1 GREY WOOL, SLIMLINE **SWEATERS** 1 CREAM CABLE STITCH 1 WOOL POLO NECK

Introduce some colour and texture with a red, grey and beige striped chunky cardigan, teamed here with the grey satin shirt and slim grey skirt.

TROUSERS GREY FLANNEL **SHIRTS** 1 WHITE SILK WITH GREY/BEIGE STRIPE, 1 GREY SATIN **CARDIGAN** CHUNKY GREY/RED STRIPE

Finding a co-ordinated wardrobe is very easy to suggest and much more difficult to achieve. There are two good ways to make it happen. One, find a clothing label that suits you in terms of cut and quality and stick with it for all your major buys. Every company has its own hand-writing which perpetuates from season to season; by being loyal to one, your wardrobe won't lurch from style to style. Two, seek out a shop where the buyer is aiming at your age-group, where the assistants are sympathetic and well-informed and can help you put your look together.

The check tweed jacket happens to be in the same fabric as the mac lining and looks smartly chic when worn together. A beige skirt, pleated from the hip to create a slimmer look, picks up the beige in the check jacket. The striped shirt and patterned floppy bow show how effective mixing stripes, checks and prints can be if you stick with the same base colours.

61

ACCESSORIES CREAM WOOL SCARF, PATTERNED SILK BOW TIE, CLASSIC JEWELLERY, CLUTCH BAG, GREY MID-HEELED SHOES

LIFESTYLES

There are two aspects of underwear that are equally important to everyone. When you are dressed you don't want your underwear to show or give even the merest hint of its existence. And when you are not, you want it to look stunningly fresh, attractive and sexy.

In fashion terms there are two currently popular looks to underwear. One is the frankly feminine appeal of lace-trimmed silk and satin bras, French knickers and camisoles. The other is a sporty, masculine mood of boxer shorts in crisp cottons, Calvin Klein-inspired briefs only just missing the Y-front and singlet vests. The two are mutually incompatible, but attractive none the less.

Whatever style you choose, eliminate the panty line on slim skirts and trousers (not the slim leg variety) by wearing French knickers or boxer shorts. Always test a new bra under a soft sweater and watch out for a smooth, natural bust shape.

Since the word thermal was revealed to mean little more than warmth, chuck out those hideous knit vests in favour of a silk camisole or spider knit vest with padded shoulders which will improve your shoulder line on sweaters enormously.

Full-length petticoats only seem to add extra bulk or an irritating lace trim that erupts in a bumpy line through shirts and sweaters but a waist petticoat is a useful possession when faced with a flimsy or sheer skirt or simply as an extra layer.

As to fabrics: silk may be luxurious, but polyester makes life with the laundry so much easier.

Camisole top and French knickers in fresh white, underwear's most useful colour. Separate cami and knickers make for greater manoeuvrability than all-in-one camiknickers.

Far left: Natural suspension with a stretch cotton strapless bra plus a pretty white waist petticoat in polyester silk and net for low-effort laundry.

Left: Lacy knit cotton vest with inset shoulder pads makes a warm, pretty extra layer and a good sweater shape. Striped boxer shorts for a sporty look and an easy skirt line.

OVER THE TOP

Whether you prefer to be cosily clad from neck to toe in warm winceyette or to slip naked between the sheets uncluttered by nighties that attempt strangulation by morning is, I think, entirely your business. I won't mention them again.

No-one, however, can exist without a dressing-gown. We need them for warmth; for lounging around at weekends; for modesty when faced with an early call from the postman or the milkman; and all the other endless housebound occupations early in the morning or late at night.

A dressing-gown is a real friend, but that doesn't permit it to be old and tatty, furry or lumpy. Dressing-gowns should have style and a degree of glamour. They must also of necessity be warm in winter and made in a practical fabric that can be easily washed.

On all these counts, a towelling robe is hard to beat. Choose a long-length style – nothing looks worse on women, just as on men, than little white legs sticking out. Men's-style dressing-gowns can also look very snazzy, especially when teamed with pyjamas in a contrasting print.

Dressing-gowns today can live dual lives. A towelling version can double as a beach cover-up, while a silky Noël Coward number can be worn to a party. That's economy.

Right: The hard-to-beat towelling robe in a fluffy white; it will wash well and looks glamorous.

Left: Tartan men's-style wrap dressing-gown teamed with spotted pyjamas.

SPECIAL OCCASIONS

Dressing to suit the occasion means covering your options or researching what's going to happen on arrival. Business or pleasure, formal or practical – clever anticipation means that all the surprises will be happy ones.

Above: Slimline skirt and satin shirt topped by a loose cardigan-style jacket, all in rich, dark colours – for town or city dwellers, this outfit goes anywhere, any time.

Unless formality is your way of life, choose an all-seasons evening dress in silk, satin or taffeta. Sleeves are wise cover for winter-tired skin or an uneven early-summer tan.

LIFESTYLES

The idea of buying a new outfit for a wedding or any special occasion that requires some real dressing up is always an exciting one. You picture yourself looking stunning, elegant, dressed if not to the nines then certainly the sixes, champagne glass in hand on some sweeping lawn.

Frustrating reality sets in when at the fourth shop that morning and twelve changes later, you've lost track of what suits you and what is, in terms of style, quite the right note to hit. Most of us dress up so infrequently that it is very easy to lose confidence and either opt for something safe and disappointingly dull or to make a flamboyant and costly mistake.

It need not be so nerve-racking. Before you start the expedition, have more than a vague idea of the colours you want to wear. More than ever you need to stick to the shades that will really bring your hair and skin tones to life to give you an extra special glow. It also makes scanning the rails a speedier and less daunting exercise.

But equally importantly, go for clothes that are very simple in their cut and their line. Avoid fussy or unnecessary trimmings or flounces. Let the fabric provide the 'special' element by either picking a wonderful print or a very rich, luxurious texture like silk, satin, silk and linen mixtures, crepe or lace.

A smashing suit in winter or summer is always a wise choice, but wear it over a simple silk T-shirt rather than a fiddly blouse or workaday collared shirt. If you need to soften the neckline wear a necklace or just a small gold chain. A silk dress or a two-piece are obviously also good options.

In Summer, uncertain British weather makes it something of a problem to plan in advance with confidence. If the day dawns dull and chilly, try adding warm under-layers like a vest, camisole, petticoat – or even all three – before you resort to covering up your new purchase with a jacket. However, it's a good idea to own a classic style jacket or blazer in a basic colour linen or cotton gabardine that will do the trick for years, if necessary.

Dispensing with tights or stockings even if your legs are wonderfully tanned will always dilute the well-groomed image. The Princess of Wales once got away with it at Ascot but any other girl who tried to enter the Royal Enclosure bare-legged would have been firmly turned away.

These seemingly fuddy-duddy old rules of dress etiquette do still make sense if your aim is to be well rather than outrageously dressed. Hats are another point. Many women try to avoid wearing a hat for a special occasion mainly because they are so unused to wearing them. But a hat, however simple, does add a glossy finishing touch. As a guideline, choose your hat colour to match your neckline (as shown in the picture) and remember: hats increase the size of your head. A tall girl can get away with a much wider brimmed hat than a shorter girl.

Dressing for special occasions in winter needs a colourful touch if your outfit is to rise above the everyday level. Here a rich red wool coat is teamed with a matching suit and blouse and topped by a beret.

Right: The smartest outfits are often the simplest styles. Here this sharp navy and white combination is pulled together by the little spot handkerchief and the black belt. The pretty hat follows the colour of the top and the shoes, not seen here, are navy.

These days you can pitch your party style where you will. Cool, sophisticated, glitzy or jokey it really doesn't matter as far as fashion goes. It's just the party spirit that counts. So dress to suit, not only the event itself but also to help your mood. Start the evening well. Leave time for all those relaxing things. Like a long and lavishly scented bath. Apply your make-up to create a stunning effect. Dress to have fun and the chances are you will.

These party pages are all about the occasions when you really want to dress up. Not about the drinks and dinner parties when a beaded sweater teamed with a pleated crepe skirt, or a silk shirt worn with a pair of suede trousers juggle day and evening style to achieve that tricky blend of smart informality.

But just as it is worth investing in one fully fledged ball gown or long evening dress, it's vital to have one or two party stand-bys hanging reassuringly in the cupboard.

From left to right: Cheeky pink and black spot dress seeks shapely wearer with a good line in repartee. Shocking pink taffeta for a girl who likes her entrances – and her exits – to be noticed. Crisp white moiré suit for anyone who knows she is a cool customer. Chic blue and black silk trimmed in rich velvet spells expensive tastes.

Traditional party prettiness given a sophisticated edge in a black and white spot taffeta off the shoulder dress.

The little black dress of the 'fifties used to fill the stand-by role admirably and became a party cliché as the safe, understated little number that would clothe you through all kinds of invitations. Today, the 'eighties update is the little black and white dress. We've learnt a thing or two in the intervening years. Unrelieved black is flattering to very few, but spice it with white in spots or a strategically placed collar or shirt front and you instantly reflect light on the face. And as any fashion photographer will tell you, there's no better way to bring a sparkle to the eyes, a freshness to the skin and a gloss to the hair.

Another solution is to find a dress with chameleon-like qualities. Start with a simple shape in a plain and preferably dark colour that can with varying accessory styles completely change its appearance on every outing. The current fashionable outline is the big V, where broad shoulders of a shift dress gently taper downwards to just below the knee.

As television's 'Dynasty' has illustrated, it's a shape that makes the most of every figure type. It looks good n virtually every evening fabric from the stiffer v ets, moirés and taffetas to the more fluid matt je eys, silks and crepes. It's worth rememberin when you are choosing any kind of evening dre hat the softer the fabric the more body reveali he dress becomes. So if you are after concea nt go for a more substantial fabric.

Accessorie t the finishing gloss and glamour on e arty outfit. Glittery or lacey tights give ext azz to a simple dress and a good pair of le or shoes, suede and patent high or mid-he e best for skirts and flat pumps for ever ousers. As a guideline, the longer your ski ower your heel height – until you reach floor , when it doesn't matter. Small fabric sho bags in velvet or satin beaded or appli ways look pretty or clutch bags in suede o do a more sophisticated job. Jewellery is nishing touch and an area where you c a lot of fun. Costume jewellery is big, b retty flamboyant at the moment with large of crystal all colours, jet and pearls ador ks, arms and ears. These big pieces are xpensive but worth the outlay as they ma t what's needed to jazz up a silk shirt for ing out straight from the office as well as m e strong party statement.

Left: Black and white for a dramatic '80s update on the little black dress. Cleverly positioned white collar and shirt front reflect light for extra sparkle. On the left: loose shirt and slim skirt form the flattering V-shaped outline, and right: the black glitter jersey dress with an unexpected hint of tailoring.

73

The brightly printed skirt teams with the
bikini top rolled down.

Inset: The same print bandeau top
worn with the baggy shorts.

The roll-up roll-down bikini with the big print shirt.

The tickets have arrived, the goldfish have been put into care and now there's just the packing to be done. So what are you going to take to wear for your two-week summer break? Travelling light with a well-planned collection of clothes is eveyone's plan – putting it into action is the difficulty.

In these three pictures you have a good example of how small and yet how versatile a capsule holiday wardrobe can be. There are just six individual pieces which can be combined in countless ways to make lots of different outfits. The big brightly printed shirt can be worn as a beach cover-up or knotted round the waist and worn with the white shorts. For a dressed-up look for the evening it can be teamed with the same print bandeau top and the skirt. The swimsuit is the roll-up roll-down kind which can be made into a one piece or a tiny bikini and the top half can work as a T-shirt with the skirt or the shorts. With the addition of a few extra T-shirts, a dress and a pair of trousers in co-ordinating colours your holiday packing can be convincingly complete in the most space-saving fashion.

75

LIFESTYLES

The easy way to plan a holiday capsule wardrobe, making sure each item earns its space in the case, is to base your selection of clothes on two or three colours that work together well. Lay out on your bed the clothes you intend taking and see just how many different outfits you can make. Seven different outfits for a 14-day holiday will mean that you only wear each one twice, so stop there and don't be tempted into taking more – especially if your days are to be spent in a swimsuit on the beach. On sight-seeing holidays you will probably need more changes, and if the weather at your destination is likely to be changeable, the odd warm sweater and extra pair of trousers won't go amiss. If you still have space in the suitcase add interesting accessories rather than more clothes – you'll have lots of time to experiment with scarves, belts and jewellery to ring the changes. High-heeled shoes are very little use on a holiday so stick with sandals, espadrilles or low-heeled mules.

Dress in layers for travel, so that you can pile on or peel off according to climate. A good jacket, chunky cotton-knit sweater or cardigan that will work as your outer layer for travel but also as an extra warm layer for cooler evenings is an important item to get right.

Here's another wardrobe plan, this time for a holiday where temperatures are likely to fluctuate. Canary yellow towelling robe makes a good beach cover-up and can double as a dressing-gown. The white cotton shorts can be worn with either the white or the yellow T-shirt and, for colder days, can be topped by the turquoise cotton-knit sweater. The blue printed cotton shirt has a matching print jacket that reverses to a plain. The skirt works with the T-shirts and the sweater, and the jacket can be worn over the shorts or the swimsuit. Add the finishing touches with a panama hat and white canvas shoes.

Main picture: The yellow towelling robe makes a perfect beach cover-up over the stripe cotton jersey swimsuit.

Inset top: The reversible print-to-plain cotton jacket has a matching print skirt.

Inset bottom: Yellow T-shirt and white shorts plus the cotton knit sweater for an extra layer.

LIFESTYLES

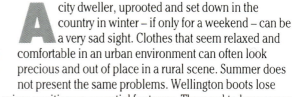

A city dweller, uprooted and set down in the country in winter – if only for a weekend – can be a very sad sight. Clothes that seem relaxed and comfortable in an urban environment can often look precious and out of place in a rural scene. Summer does not present the same problems. Wellington boots lose their prime position as essential footwear. The need to keep warm at all costs does not seem so pressing and bright primary colours or sophisticated shades which look so brash in a wintry countryside of muted tones, appear natural and fresh alongside nature's own vibrant summer colours. Winter weekends in the country need much more thought if you are going not only to look the part but also enjoy yourself.

As with any other invitation or trip it's a good idea to discover from your host or hostess just what you're likely to be doing, so that you can pack accordingly. But you won't go far wrong if you plan to spend most of your time dressed in traditional country classics, and if they have a well-worn, friendly feel about them so much the better. Shetland or Aran sweaters, cord trousers or knickerbockers, jeans, plaid or tweedy skirts, all look at home in the country. A good warm and preferably waterproof coat or jacket is a necessity plus of course those inevitable wellies. Don't forget outdoor accessories either, like scarves, gloves and a hat with an individual, crumpled air to keep the extremities warm. Remember anything too new looks totally out of place in the country!

Still sticking to the maxim that travelling light is a good thing, keep the size of your weekend bag within bounds by taking a few items that work together well, such as a yellow cable chunky knit sweater which can be worn with a skirt or breeches; a plaid pleated skirt, to be dressed down with a sweater and up with a red silk shirt; socks, tights, scarf, wellies and two-toned brogues. And find room for a hot water bottle – you won't regret it!

Old, comfortable and classic may be the key adjectives for roam-about everyday clothes but townies should never underestimate the alacrity with which country cousins dress up, often on the slimmest of excuses. An invitation to Sunday lunch means changing out of your jeans and into something a good deal smarter. My rule, backed by experience rather than statistics, is that the further north you go the more formally you should dress for drinks, lunch or dinner invitations. So make sure your packing has left you prepared for such eventualities.

CHECKLIST ■ **TROUSERS** GREEN CORD BREECHES **SKIRT** PLAID PLEATED **SWEATER** CHUNKY YELLOW CABLE KNIT **SHIRT** RED SILK

Country double act for a winter weekend. Dressed in an Aran sweater, proofed cotton mac, tough cord breeches and matching socks, she combines style and practical warmth. His outfit has the same 'Sloane' qualities, a famous Barbour jacket worn with cord trousers and the inevitable green wellies.

■ **FOOTWEAR** GREEN WELLINGTON BOOTS, BROGUE SHOES **ACCESSORIES** TIGHTS, SOCKS, SCARF **ESSENTIAL** HOT WATER BOTTLE

CHECKLIST ■ **TO WEAR** 1 SUIT, 1 SHIRT, 1 PAIR OF SHOES ■ **TO PACK** 1 SHIRT, 1 SILK SHIRT, 1 KIMONO DRESSING GOWN,

For an overnight business trip you want to travel light. One basic suit in a good quality fabric and a dark colour will see you through the journey, a working dinner and a morning meeting. Don't economize on the shirt space in your travel bag. This bright yellow shirt livens up the grey suit skirt for a working dinner on arrival.

When travelling on business organize your clothes with particular care so that not only will they give you the feeling of confidence you need if meeting associates for the first time, but also fit neatly into a small overnight bag.

Unless you have to attend a formal evening function (check this out in advance), one suit – in a smart, dark colour and of good-quality fabric – will see you through the journey, a working dinner and a morning meeting. Rely on shirts to ring the changes. Take a spare for the following morning and one to change into for dinner – something like a plain, lively coloured silk that will look bright and feminine. In winter, a soft sweater or cardigan will be more comfortable to travel in than a jacket and provide an extra layer of warmth.

A cotton or silk kimono makes a less bulky cover-up than a dressing gown. Pack extra tights as essential insurance against accidents with fingernails. Regular travellers should keep a washbag at the ready with miniature bottles of shampoo, cleanser and so on, and don't be tempted to use it between trips or you will defeat your purpose. Separate dirty laundry from clean clothes in a drawstring bag (saves endless embarrassment in customs, too!).

81

■ 1 NIGHTIE, CHANGE OF UNDIES, 3 PAIRS TIGHTS, 1 PAIR OF SHOES, 1 WASHBAG, 1 HAIRDRIER WITH A PLUG, 1 LAUNDRY BAG

Health within means outer beauty. A body nourished by fresh foods and toned up with enjoyable exercise feels good and looks better. Make-up provides the final gloss on this natural attractiveness, with beautiful cosmetic colours lightly applied and gently blended.

Healthy skin is glowing and supple. A good skin-care routine and a diet including lots of fresh fruit and vegetables gives you bare-faced confidence to welcome sun, wind and moisture.

Above: A soft blush can be pretty even when it's a sign of embarrassment – but don't forget blushing also means pleasure, excitement, a sense of achievement. Pearly pinks highlighting lips, cheeks and eyes create an intriguing warmth behind the cool exterior.

Blondes should always aim to keep their make-up looking light. Harsh bright colours applied with too heavy a hand produce hard results ...pletely at odds with the ...acy of blonde colouring. If ... eyes are blue or grey and ... skin tone pink, base your ...tte of make-up colours on ... blue shades. If your eyes ...pen to be hazel or light ...wn shades, however, your ...dows, blushers and ...ticks can afford to be ...mer, with just a hint of ...ow in their composition.
...undation Should be as ...fect as possible a match to ...r natural skin tone. Always ...t a colour on neck or face – a ...nd or wrist won't give you an ...curate reading.
...usher Powdery pink, dusty ro.se and raspberry for pinky skin tones. Tawny pink and peachy pink for golden tones.
Eyes Grey-blues, slate greys, rose-pinks, grey-greens, soft browns, lemon-yellows.
Lips All shades of bluey pinks or reds. Warmer skin tones can wear peach pink or light red.
Mascara Brown, slate grey, blue or violet.

BLENDER TIP ONE
Learn how to blend colour and texture and you have the key to a perfect make-up. Foundation will always be easier to apply if your skin is well moisturized. First, dot foundation all over your face and then smooth it over your skin with a just-damp sponge for a wonderfully natural and even finish. Blend just under the jaw line – never down the neck. Pat or press concealer on to any dark areas under eyes or on the sides of your nose.

Here the subtle daytime make-up gets an extra boost for an evening look emphasizing eyes and lips. The eyes are outlined with smokey grey pencil smoothly blended in; dusty pink shadow covers the lid and extends to the outer corner of the eye where it blends into soft pink blusher; deep mauve shadow sweeps from the inner corner into the eye socket. The lips are outlined then filled in with frosty deep pink.

Left: A pink-based delicate daytime make-up for a grey or blue-eyed blonde.

The right tools will help you do each job with finesse. Use a small cosmetic sponge, slightly damp to apply foundation and a soft, fat brush to dust powder over face, eyelids and lips.

85

Brown, silver and violet give eyes a smouldering look for evening. Silver highlights the brow bone, *frosty brown covers the socket and violet defines the eyes. Lips and blusher reflect a metallic brown hue.* *Right: A light daytime look for a brunette uses pinky blusher and blue/grey eyeshadow.*

A s with clothes, the dark-haired girl will maximize her looks and style if the colours she applies to her face are the cool, strong shades – carefully blended of course. Wishy washy pastels will only weaken her features. Brunettes with pale skins often make the mistake of picking a foundation several shades darker than their natural tone – the result is always an over-made-up unnatural look. Blusher cleverly applied is a much more effective way to add colour to pale skin and bring life to your features.

Foundation Should be a perfect match to your natural skin tone. Always test a colour on neck or face.

Blusher Blue-pink, tawny pink or light wine shades.

Eyes All browns, navy, violet, coral, dark green, silver, gold and grey.

Lips Clear reds, cherry, burgundy, fuchsia, metallic brown.

Mascara Black, black/brown, brown, dark blue or green.

BLENDER TIP TWO

The effect of blusher should always be subtle. Blusher is for bringing a glow to the skin, not a means of shaping the face, so don't draw on a hard-edged wedge of colour. Powder blusher is the easiest type to apply, using a generously sized brush. Start with just a little – you can always add more – and blend in colour to the apples of your cheeks, stroking colour up to your brow-bone. Brushing in a figure-of-eight motion is a good method. Finish by checking your profile view.

86

After your blusher has been well blended, re-powder your face.

Redheads should stick to the warm, yellow-based shades for skin, eyes and lips if they want a natural and complimentary make-up. The blue-based tones that crop up in all true pinks will jar with their colouring, leaving an onlooker with the impression of lipstick rather than lips or blusher as opposed to a skin glowing with health. If you have freckles, don't try to cover them up with a heavy foundation. Treat them as the asset they are, not the liability they were once thought to be, by using a light and translucent base.

Foundation Should be a perfect match to your natural skin tone. Always test a colour on neck or face.

Blusher Peach, apricot, amber or cinnamon.

Eyes Moss, olive, emerald green, rust, gold, copper, teal, gold, mustard or aquamarine.

Lips Peach, coral, orange, brick red, or cinnamon.

Mascara Brown or bottle green.

Left: A natural peach-based daytime make-up.

To prepare the daytime make-up into a bolder evening look always cleanse and re-apply your foundation. Amber was used for blusher, with a gold and amber mix on the lips. A light peachy gold covers the whole eyelid area, while a deeper amber defines the eye. Deep aqua green is blended into the socket and brushed outwards to the brow bone.

Use a brush carefully and slowly to blend the colours softly into one another.

Finally apply mascara to lashes top and bottom. Two light coats are better than one heavy one. Separate the lashes with a lash comb for a natural look.

BLENDER TIP THREE
Eye colour needs careful blending to be effective. Remember that light colours advance and darker shades retreat. First brush a light colour shadow over the eyelid blending it evenly up to the eyebrow; outline and blend a darker shade into the socket up on to the brow bone, and under the bottom lashes; outline the eye with pencil and smudge the line for a softer look; mascara comes last.

89

LIFESTYLES

Dark-skinned brunettes look their best keeping to cool strong colours for lips, cheeks and eyes. Since most have a complexion which is uneven in tone, they need a concealer to lighten dark areas under eyes and around the nostrils, as well as a darker cover-up to disguise differences in pigmentation elsewhere on the face. Too matt a finish has a heavy or deadening effect on the skin, so pick a foundation with a bronze glow for a healthy sheen and go easy on the powder. Lips too need careful treatment.

Foundation Natural skin tone with bronze highlights.
Blusher Bright pink or red; burgundy, plum.
Eyes Teal, dark brown, peacock blue, navy, burgundy, plum violet, mauve. (All colours lose some of their brightness once on.)
Lips All blue pinks, clear red, burgundy, plum, cherry.
Mascara Black, brown/black, navy, purple.

BLENDER TIP FOUR

Like the complexion, lips are likely to be uneven in tone; the upper lip, for example, is usually darker than the lower one. Choose a selection of lipstick colours and blend them together with a brush to achieve a uniform effect. First outline the lips with either a pencil or a brush, and then fill in with a brush carefully blending the lip line with the lip colour. Blot with a tissue and finally add more lip colour or gloss. A lip line will help prevent lipstick from bleeding. Don't be tempted to draw your lip line outside or inside the natural one.

90

A dramatic blend of peacock blue and violet for sultry evening eyes. Bright fuchsia lips with a carefully blended outline tone with a blue-pink glossy blusher brushed high on the cheekbones.

To minimize a full mouth use a darker shade in the centre of the lips. To maximize a small or thin mouth use a paler shade in the centre.

Right: A light daytime make-up with soft shades of brown for eyes and raspberry red for lips.

Fashionstyles

Fashions – or at least, fashionable details like the length of a hem, the fullness of a skirt, or passion for a particular colour – may come and go, but certain looks or styles are always with us. Whether because they are unfailingly flattering or because they appeal to a deep need to present oneself in a particular way, these are the styles that will always have their devoted exponents.

In the following pages we turn the spotlight on nine of the styles in fashion that can be trusted to endure – though not without adaptation to the spirit of the hour. For nothing stands still in the world of fashion, and there's a world of difference between cultivating the look that suits you best and getting stuck in a rut. Women – especially those with style – gain enormous pleasure from choosing clothes, not only because of the satisfaction that comes from 'getting it right' but also from playing with clothes that express their personality (or personalities). If you want to be a jetsetter today and a second-hand Rose tomorrow, go ahead. Here's who they are, and how they do it . . .

Everything about the executive style speaks of success. This girl's clothes are both sharp and feminine but unfussy. She chooses up-to-date classics, superbly made in high-class fabrics that she matches with gilt-edged grooming. Her appearance has to be one of her great assets, and she knows it.

Today's executive no longer hides behind a dull grey tailored suit and stiff white shirt. Her clothes are stylish but not shocking, with comfort a high priority.

Left: An easy jersey dress with a strong shoulder line and dolman sleeves sees her colourfully through a busy day.

Above: The dress slips easily under a comfortable coat of hardworking beige gaberdine when she's out on appointments or on her travels.

FASHIONSTYLES

Relaxed in line, easy to wear but very together separates. Co-ordinating colours unite tailored trousers and textured knit jacket in dignified brown sharpened up by a dazzling white shirt.

96

The girl who chooses to dress 'executive style' usually has good reason for doing so. She would look out of place in the country; downright peculiar knee-deep in nappies and washing-up and miscast running a cottage industry. For she is either at the top of her chosen business or professional career or is firmly intent on getting there.

Research done in the United States has shown that over 75 per cent of the initial impact a person makes is entirely visual. It's how you look, not how you speak or even what you say, that forms those vital first impressions. That's useful information for anyone, but crucial for any woman bent on a successful career. Dressing the part of an efficient, organized and discerning woman is half the battle won. You can opt for a unisex uniform or strict suit and shirt where the only feminizing touch is a bow at the neck rather than a tie. But as it becomes increasingly usual to find women in key posts the necessity of adopting a masculine style as camouflage is no longer an aid to survival. It eventually loses you the advantage points to be gained by allowing more individuality, personality and femininity into the way you dress. You have to be certain of course, that the messages transmitted by your self-presentation are the right ones.

In this endeavour, there are some obvious pitfalls to avoid. However much you love fashion, steer clear of its weirder flights of fantasy. You want to be noticed for yourself as a complete entity, not simply for your oddball taste in clothes. Choose colours and prints carefully, and reject the garish. Sticking to cool or dark colours is best, although the occasional primary splash can be effective.

Dressing the part of an efficient, organized and discerning woman is half the battle won

The cloth of executive woman's coat is superb in quality. Classically cut in beige gaberdine, it's generous enough to work over all her clothes. The ultimate in layer dressing, it slips on and off with minimum fuss – perfect for comfortable travelling, over a soft sweater and tailored trousers, equally at ease over the shapely suit. The hat's for impact, small and snappy.

Anyone who pulls off 'executive style' with panache understands how to use colour to full advantage. It's essential to build up a wardrobe of clothes that all work together so that getting dressed every morning is a quickly accomplished task. The surest way to achieve this is to limit severely the number of different colours in her wardrobe. She will choose one or two basics such as navy or grey, black or brown and make all major purchases in that shade, only occasionally splashing out on a bright or a pastel to add a lift.

By sticking with her colour plan over a period of years, not simply one or two seasons, she will be able to buy the high quality, high cost clothes that endorse her successful image. Buy less but spend more is her credo. She chooses her styles carefully, knowing that today's snappy classics in fine fabrics have the right look and the staying power. She'll avoid trimmings and fiddly details because not only will they date but also spoil her characteristically uncluttered style. Jewellery s played down to a minimum of good pieces luring the day, with no distracting bangles or angling necklaces.

She chooses her styles carefully, knowing that today's snappy classics in fine fabrics have the right look and the staying power

You may often find her wearing a suit, but it will be built on feminine not masculine lines, either single or double breasted, with rounded collar or soft revers plus a skirt that is super slim or in fluid pleats. She will team it with a silk or satin shirt or classic sweater. The suit may be tailored, but it will never be tight, allowing her to work and move easily and comfortably.

Separates can fit in to executive style if they have the right degree of formality. She may have a cardigan jacket to wear with a shirt and skirt or well-cut trousers; she may look good in cleverly co-ordinated knitwear; but separates usually only work when colour matched in a deliberate way, to reach the required level of smartness.

Dresses can be difficult for the stylish executive, often looking either drab and matronly or too youthfully girlish. The simple lambswool or cashmere knit sweater dress, however, or the classic shirt-style coat dress have neither of these drawbacks yet always look sophisticated.

Left: Pale beige and very interesting, a straight and narrow suit with a high but shapely waistband and casual side pockets in the skirt, is teamed with a cardigan of gentle peach, finished with a neat collar and impeccable stitching. Accessories underline the message without distracting from it.

Above: For warmer days, a silky tobacco brown shirt with round collar looks good.

99

FASHIONSTYLES

While other mortals occasionally go to parties, the executive's life is packed with functions. Just another word for work, but they frequently take place out of strict working hours and for women require a clever brand of dressed-down dressing-up.

Getting the balance right is tricky. Executive woman steers clear of anything too flimsy or flirtatious, anything obviously sexy or too party-party. She prefers simply shaped dresses in stunning fabrics like jewel-coloured satin, printed silks or usefully ubiquitous black crepe and jersey. Or if the timing of the function means going on straight from the office she will start her day wearing the kind of skirt that can be speedily transformed by the addition of a beautiful evening shirt and glitzy jewellery.

When the object of the campaign is self-presentation, point one is to be super-meticulous about grooming. Choose a hairstyle that not only suits you but also your type of hair, so that it can be maintained with the greatest ease. Make the time at the beginning of the day to put your make-up on with care so that it needs only minor repairs thereafter. Buy your tights in bulk so that you are never without an unladdered or unscagged pair. It's better not to wear nail polish than risk the chance of a scruffy looking chip. Finally, clothes maintenance is so important. Neglected shoes, unpressed suits or shirts that look less than spanking fresh will only let you down. For as the successful executive dresser knows, an untidy appearance implies − heaven forbid − an untidy and disorganized mind.

Left: For dressing up after dark, the glamour of this stunningly simple dress is in the fabric, strong blue gleaming out of black. The V-shape is slick and flattering, drawing attention to meticulously presented face and hairstyle. And no fussy jewellery, just big bold blue earrings.

When six p.m. means a dramatic change of scene, a pleated skirt of black crepe easily switches roles. Effect the transformation with a fabulous shirt of purple satin, an enormous glossy bow at the neckline emphasized with ropes of glittering beads.

Comfortably clad for a deskbound day in a far-from ordinary knitted cardigan in dark taupe, styled to perfection over a white silk blouse.

EXECUTIVE

WISE **A**ND **W**ITTY

Leather gloves are unconstricting, feel good and last well: fur at the wrist is a wise and witty touch. One essential is a superb watch: immediately readable, the crocodile strap hinting at distinction. If specs are needed they'll be assertive and modern, good-looking in their own right while fitting in with the working wardrobe.

Executive woman counts tabletop technology among her valued delegates. Nothing here that is no known to be useful and believed to be beautiful, from ultraslim typewriter to leatherbound Filofax. She devotes as much attention to her choice of fashion accessories as she does to office equipment. Everything earns its place by co-ordinating cleverly with everything else, while reflecting a distinctively female touch in interesting textures, rounded lines and smoothness of finish.

STAPLE **I**TEMS

An executive doesn't have time to waste switching bags for every outfit. She relies on staple items, and for them, part of the job is maintaining the image. A wooden attaché case — durable and smooth to the touch — doubles up as a kneetop desk in trains and planes and dares to be impressively different. The crocodile bag can be hand-held or slipped on the shoulder. Capacious but easy to handle, its classy looks can only improve with time. Ubiquitous, yes; anonymous, no: tapestry-fronted Filofax stands out from the crowd.

PRACTICAL **P**LANNING

Is it good fortune or good planning that the most practical, medium-heel court shoes in beige suede also make legs look longer, ankles slimmer? Clever black leather 'bucket' bag holds everything from car keys to credit cards and never falls over.

DYNASTY

Day and night this strictly female female exudes a ritzy glamour. Long before the American super soaps gave her an 'eighties stamp she was the Vamp, decidedly dangerous to know. But with the introduction of pliant Krystle and saccharine Pam, even good girls can glitter.

Smouldering by day in a moulded leather skirt with pop studs up the back, the red satin shirt flaunts a flamboyant bow on the collar; the fur and jewels show we are talking serious money.

Above: Even a subtle creamy knit gets the treatment. The slim stretchy knitted skirt stops short at the knee and clings to perfect contours. The shawl collar and big shoulders give the characteristic V-silhouette.

Lavishly embodied as this style now is by the ladies of 'Dynasty' and 'Dallas', they did not create it but simply mirrored a look that has been with us for decades and will flourish still when the soaps have bubbled away. From the top of her elaborately coiffured head, to the tip of her perfectly varnished toes she has deliberated on every detail of her look, and is well-satisfied with the result.

Sex and money are the two vital elements in her style, but with a particular emphasis of her own. The figure-hugging clothes in touch-me fabrics are often blatantly sexy, but the strong square shoulders give the message that any encounter will be on her terms: she is ultra-feminine, but with power – not a melting little number to be bent to his will. Her impact is precisely gauged: turned down to a discreet undercurrent for meeting the bank manager, in the evening switched up to full power when she meets a new man who claims her attention.

When money is no object clothes do not have to be low-key, versatile or practical. She can buy a dynamic outfit to be worn only once for a specific occasion. She would die if an acquaintance had seen any of her clothes often enough to say, 'I've *always* loved that suit.' What's more, this is new money, and it's still being deliciously savoured. Old money might send granny's mink to be mended and re-modelled; new money wants this season's fur, bought with a particular outfit in mind.

There are two distinct breeds of Dynasty women: those that want to work and those that don't. Both make a positive choice. The Dynasty businesswoman is quite a new phenomenon. She still allows herself to look

Left: This lady means business and conducts it in an outfit that leaves no room for doubt about who runs the company. The suit is almost classic, but the shoulders are sharper, the skirt tighter; the hat and cerise shirt are typically head-turning.

Right: Sunset strip – almost. The velvet, off-the-shoulder dress is short, gathered at the back with a bow, and worn with sheer black stockings

sexy, but she is ultra-sharp too. A dazzling mixture of femininity and aggression, she won't let anyone push her around.

But whether she works or not, this woman always looks particularly stunning during the day. Her faultless, almost ostentatious, good grooming is far more noticeable when those around her have made no more than a perfunctory effort, and her careful co-ordination of bold colours means that she never goes anywhere without making a tremendous impact on everyone – male and female. Her glossy, supremely confident look carries all before her. You don't have to be a beauty to have glamour but you must work hard at it. If there is any hint of slovenliness then the high-octane sexiness is in danger of being reclassified as tarty.

This woman never looks casual. Jeans, in her opinion, are for men. She does not believe clothes were meant to be comfortable. Choosing a tracksuit or a jumpsuit because it was easy to wear is something that would never cross her mind. Like everything else in this life, clothes have work to do, and hers are an absolutely essential part of her image.

Dynasty woman lives for the evening when she can really go to town on colour and style. It is difficult, if not impossible to outshine a Dynasty lady at night. The worst thing that could possibly happen to her would be to pass unnoticed at a party. For this reason anything that smacks of quiet good taste is absolutely out. Dynasty doesn't flow or drape discreetly – it billows, makes sharp angles or is outrageously revealing. In one way or another it calls for your attention.

The Dynasty woman has body skin like satin, with a gold sheen: it is endlessly bathed, anointed, pampered, exercised and pummelled. She would never let herself get out of shape – but if there was a part of her body that she considered less than perfect she would have the good sense to keep it cleverly covered, or draw attention from it with emphasis elsewhere. Well-padded shoulders have more than one function: they also make the waist look correspondingly tiny. Giant bows or outrageous detailing can give a more primly tailored costume as much impact as the revealing cut-away

Sex and money are the two vital elements in her style, but with a particular emphasis of her own

FASHIONSTYLES

The vamp-turned-Dynasty woman doesn't worry to the same degree as other expensive dressers about designer names or the latest fashion trends. Whatever they might be saying in Paris, this woman wants a cut that shows off her body and hugs its contours, that plays up her good points and minimizes the bad. Experience has taught her that a very definite silhouette works best for most of her clothes. Best of all is the V-shape – the broad shoulders and the very slim hips. The rest depends on how good her natural equipment is: if she has got a good bosom she will display it; a tiny waist will be clinched in as small as it will go, and if she has seemingly endless, model-girl legs no opportunity to show them off will be wasted.

So, if the trend is for the baggy or the utilitarian, she will let other women become fashion slaves, going her own sweet way and buying what she knows suits her best.

The fabrics she prefers tend to shine. If it is silk, it will be silk with a definite sheen; satin's even better. Apart from anything else, shiny materials are sexy, emphasizing body-line more than a matt fabric can. She also likes the feel and connotations of leather, especially when cut tightly in figure-hugging style. Furs, of course, are liked for their wickedly luxurious feel as well as for being status symbols. Texture is very important: only the softest wools, such as cashmere, are worn; and the suppleness and strokeable softness of suede is an acceptable alternative to the bolder slickness of shiny leather.

This is the look that can be most successfully copied by women who don't have endless money to spend. In the final analysis this is a style that stands or falls on instant impact. The hidden detail, the secret marks of quality, count for nothing if heads don't turn the moment this woman walks into the room. An approximation of the right cut and a bold use of colour and design can produce an outfit almost as good as the real thing if carried off with confidence and panache. She might be a born up-stager, but she is less of a snob than most, and if your outfit catches more eyes than hers, she will find it cold comfort that hers cost twice as much.

Above: The knotted sarong and T-shirt made glamorous by being made in cobalt-blue silk, and worn with a suite of important jewellery. To show how little she cares, that necklace is worn under the shirt

Right: This magnificent silver fox coat is what she slips over her silk suit to go shopping. With its Zhivago hat it's right for the kind of impressive jewellery she prefers

The evening dress par excellence: yards of shimmering crepe de chine hug the body then billow out, the better to enhance her slightest movement. A wrap around the neck frames the face and emphasizes what is left bare elsewhere.

DYNASTY Accessories

A WAVE OF THE HAND

One of the few women who still cares to wear gloves, she needs dozens of pairs, not because she wants to keep her hands warm, but because each outfit calls for something special to finish it off: some are for day, some are for evening, some wrist length, some to the elbow, in leather, suede, silk or trimmed with fur, and beautifully stitched.

A PERFECT MATCH

Whatever the time or the occasion, bags will match shoes closely, and will often be designed, perhaps with a decorative motif, to do so. The tiny sculptured bag, held in an exquisitely manicured hand, serves, like the chunky bracelet, to emphasize her every gesture. The total effect of such close co-ordination is very compelling.

SUPPORTING ROLES

Even the bit-players are chosen with care. She needs few items in her handbag — a little compact, elegant lipstick case, mirror and perfume spray — so a capacious bag is unnecessary as well as carrying irrelevant associations of practicality. She almost always chooses a clutch bag, though she may add a long gold chain to turn it into a shoulder bag when she needs one hand for the champagne and another for the canapés.

The Dynasty woman chooses accessories that are sexy, particularly her stockings (not tights) and probably her jewellery. She believes in highlighting outfits with unusual detail, and if this is not integral to the garment she will certainly add it on in the shape of an interesting belt, brooch, or impossible hat. If her outfit is quiet, it is because she's got some dramatic accessories to do the talking.

Left: What more appropriate detail to attend to than a well-turned ankle? Slender golden threads on these very high-heeled shoes echo the motif on the back. Glittery stockings, of course.

ACCENTUATE THE POSITIVE

The way this lady wears them, belts are a very sexy fashion extra, emphasizing her curves while co-ordinating — or contrasting skilfully — with her outfit, perhaps picking up an unexpected detail like the trimming on her gloves. She likes opulent buckles and sparkling stones set into the band — a way of shining brightly even before the lights go down. Belts in bright tones of leather or suede enable her to indulge her fondness for emphatic colours.

113

COUNTRY

Our romantic imaginings about life in the country focus on an idealized place where muddy boots and weatherproof garments do not exist. The extremely feminine woman who adorns herself with the country look is more often to be found in the heart of town than down on the farm.

Right: Heathery shades soften the look of a tailored suit, given the romantic air with lace handkerchief and a brooch at the high neck – and by the fact that it's a touch too long to be practical.

Above: A strict check shirt and figure-hugging waistcoat could look mannish on someone else, but with a scarf tied in a bow at the neck, the blend of naturally gentle colours, and the comforting softness of Viyella country girl looks as vulnerably feminine as usual.

Above: Favourites from the treasure chest: creamy silk brocade waistcoat sprigged with pink, a characteristic cameo at the neck of an antique blouse.

Right: Both the smock and the pinafore are dear to the country girl's heart: in forest green, over a full sleeved and fanciful creamy shirt, the look is wonderfully simple.

The woman who wears the country look should not be confused with the country girl who works on the land, or even the one who loves rambling, hunting or other country pursuits. While she *may* take part in all or any of these things, it is not very likely, and her personal style is influenced by quite different considerations. There is something passive and gentle about her: she would prefer to wait at home to greet the outdoor types on their return. It follows that there is nothing particularly sensible nor practical about what she wears — none of her favourite clothes would withstand much exposure to unfriendly elements, and her outfits are put together with too much thought and care for her to risk spoiling the look with activity of a hearty kind. Neither is there anything rough-weave, homespun or 'self-sufficient' about her style.

Her country look is inspired by everything that is aesthetically pleasing, gentle, benign and prettily traditional about country life. It is cottagey and peaceful — Wordsworth's view of rural bliss rather than the harsher realities of Thomas Hardy. It is spring and autumn; soft, harmonious colours, birdsong and the intricate patterns of hedgerows.

There is a timeless quality to her look. It mixes Victorian and Edwardian unselfconsciously with other influences from the past — Jane Austen heroines and Dresden shepherdesses — and in some ways it is resistant to fashion. The overall shape, look and feel endure recognizably whatever the fashion climate, but of course it inevitably bears some of the marks of the era in which it finds itself. This happens most notably in the smaller details: a whisper of net on a bowler hat, for instance, is a fashion conceit that she will adore for a time, but may not stay the course to become a standard part of the look.

Her clothes are usually fairly long, as you would expect from the period she prefers. They are either loose and romantic in shape, or tailored and fitted — though they are never clinging or overtly sexy. She looks at her most endearing and gamine in boyishly tailored clothes, never more feminine than when the cut is at its most severe. She also especially likes to wear traditional dresses and comfortable clothes — though she would never feel happy in anything really casual.

She has an irresistibly girlish quality; there is nothing very knowing or sophisticated about her style of dressing. She has as much man-appeal as the more womanly female and an apparently unwitting sexiness. The fact that she rarely reveals more than a well-turned ankle, and is otherwise usually primly covered right up to the neck and past the wrist can make her more tantalizing to many men than the woman who displays her assets. This is partly because her personality matches the traditional look of her clothes. She is a pliant female who wants to be looked after and told what to do, and has great respect for old-time values and virtues. She brings out the protective male in her admirers, and is never known to be aggressive or strident.

There is a sense in which the woman who wears this look really loves her clothes. That is because she tends to gravitate towards garments with a history. A lot of what she wears is genuinely old and she enjoys speculating about the past history of favourite pieces. What she likes best of all is an item that has been in the family, such as Granny's nightdress or Uncle Albert's waistcoat. She will, of course, wear them in a way that would faintly scandalize her forebears if they knew: Granny's nightdress would be more likely to take her out in the evening than to see her safely tucked up in bed.

Her country look is inspired by everything that is aesthetically pleasing, gentle, benign and prettily traditional

Most of her main items, such as suits and skirts and coats, are likely to be new, but with the cut that gives a period feel combined with an up-to-date slant. It is her accessories, shirts, and smaller items that tend to be old and beautifully preserved. She will be very excited if she can find knitwear in mint condition, though this happens less often than she would hope. Fortunately there are still plenty of examples of cotton, lace and silk as she would like, if she is prepared to hunt for them. She gives a new lease of life to antique underwear, such as petticoats, and is good at utilizing odd pieces of lace as handkerchiefs, jabots and bows — especially such pieces as old lace dressing-table runners. She appreciates traditional workmanship, such as intricate smocking and complicated Fair Isle, and cherishes the buttons to be found on old blouses and the infinite variety of lace.

FASHIONSTYLES

The fabrics the country girl chooses always have a soft and comfortable feel to them. Some are naturally soft, such as Viyella, pure wools, velvet and suede. Others are worn into softness even if they started out new and stiff, such as cord, plaid, and antique cottons. Her nostalgia for a dreamy romantic past means that she rather despises the obviously new and crisp, much preferring anything that is aged and well worn. She values all things that have stood the test of time, and when it comes to clothes, thinks they look and feel nicer when they are worn in. Warm, soft fabrics are a perfect foil for a stiff collar, pert frill or cuffs that have been newly starched.

The combinations of colours she prefers are also soft and harmonious. If one colour exemplifies this look it would be pink — an old dusty rose colour with warmth and depth. But the country girl does not go for the obviously pretty-pretty. Her charm is more subtle and cleverly expressed. So it is that she also likes autumnal collections of burnished gold, browns, deep reds, and heathery mixtures of greens, lilacs and purples. She wears the occasional touch of white, such as a bleached and restored piece of old lace masquerading as a handkerchief tucked casually into a pocket, or wound round her neck. But on the whole she prefers off-white, creams and the parchment tones of whites that have faded with the years.

She would never be seen in efficient 'man-made' colours, such as black, navy or grey, which are too determined to suit her style. The cottagey, country look that she puts together so well is essentially softer — and slightly fussy too. That is why she is in love with prints, which she mixes together in a confident way. She is unmoved by bold zig-zag stripes or knockout spots, or anything with a modern feel in style or colouring. She likes traditional patterns, particularly those that are small and delicate in design. Interwoven flowers and leaves are a favourite motif, as are the complicated, tiny geometric patterns reminiscent of snowflakes and leaf forms that make up traditional Fair Isle designs.

Above: The warm red and soft velvet of this dress is a combination the country girl adores for the evening. But what marks out this dress as hers are the puffed sleeves, deep highwayman cuffs, and the girlish polka-dot fabric interweaved to soften the otherwise plain sophistication of the dress.

Her nostalgia for a dreamy romantic past means that she rather despises the obviously new and crisp

Unmistakeably the smock of the shepherdess, but with exceptional details – the Puritan collar, pin-tucked bodice and intricate stitching, all adding up to creamy innocence.

FASHIONSTYLES

*S*he will often accessorize with a little family of treasures she has collected

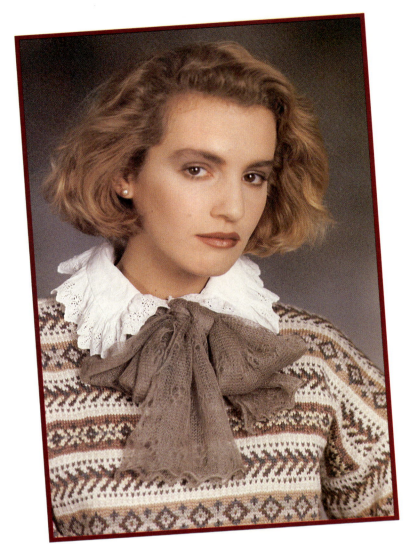

Right: Country girl mixes texture and colour to achieve a thoroughly original look. Characteristic white lace collar brightens an almost-too-subtle heathery Fair Isle. There's a touch of genius in the lace bow.

Opposite: Beautifully warm, still her sheepskin jacket is cut to curve, the numerous and unusually small buttons feminizing the look while performing their task. Over a skirt that's almost ankle length the proportions are perfect. Hats with a brim are appropriate, enhancing her shyness of manner.

*A*t its best, this look is distinguished by the original way disparate items are put together. Gathering bits and pieces from different periods and knowing how to combine them is a particular talent. Where this shows most effectively is in her choice of accessories. Her look is influenced by the Victorian approach to collections. In the same way that they liked to group clusters of gilt-framed miniatures, and china ornaments, so she will often accessorize with a little family of treasures. Or if her accessories are few, she will go for those that are patterned rather than plain, intricate rather than bold.

The idea of wearing a dress without putting her particular stamp on it is unthinkable. She will soften with frills, emphasize with a hat − which she loves any excuse to wear, from perky bowlers to dairymaid straw − and hang with pretty earrings, cameos and brooches. Gloves, especially antique

gloves, often form part of her look, as do patterned stockings. She also prefers bags that are 'finds' such as embroidered silk evening bags and tapestried carpet bags. She likes stick pins and hat pins, and unusual costume jewellery that is pretty rather than dramatic. The eclectic look may never be smart, but smartness is not something to which she aspires.

In keeping with her look, the country girl keeps her make-up simple. She usually goes for subtle natural colours, but if she needs to make more of an impact, may choose a bright mouth and pinkish blusher. Her hair is fresh, gleaming and well-cut, but never elaborately styled. She lets it fall the way it wants to go so that it can look tousled, but not artfully so. When she wears nail varnish it is shell pink, on nails that she never allows to grow very long. She likes scents that are pure flower essences, sometimes wafting a trail of rose-petals and lavender − as her grandmother did.

COUNTRY Accessories

LITTLE GIRL LOST

The little-girl-lost drooping petticoat, woolly, flower-patterned stockings and sensible brown suede shoes have an endearing air.

She would feel lost without her capacious tapestry bag, with everything she needs safe inside, and it has the texture, colours and pattern she adores.

COLOUR TOUCHES

When the weather is chilly, a shawl is very much her style. She will have a number of fabric remnants in all colours and patterns that she can wear in this way. Though warm and practical, her gloves are chosen as much for colour as usefulness.

RECURRING THEMES

A favourite way to wear old lace is to tie it round her neck in a bow to emphasize the high lace collar of a shirt.

Lace-up ankle boots (or buttoned boots) recall the Victorian schoolroom, a theme that runs through her wardrobe.

The country girl often chooses her accessories with more care than the larger items in her wardrobe, enraptured as she is by little details. She has boxes of exquisite little pieces, a hat for every occasion, and a drawer of fabric pieces that can be twisted, tied, thrown over or pinned to an outfit to make it look quite different. She prefers the antique, but will adapt a modern item to give it the twist she prefers.

Left: The bowler could look severe but she makes it quirkily romantic by casually pinning a veil of black net to the brim.

123

She's a girl on the move. You
can't keep her still for long.
She has boundless energy
that demands release, wearing clothes
that allow her the freedom to run,
dance and play at will. Her style is
always casual; she loathes dressing
up, preferring clothes that are
crisp and uncontrived.

ACTION GIRL

*In summer, the comfort and stretch of cotton
jersey makes it a fabric favourite, seen here in a
striped bandeau top and leggings and roomy
golfer cardigan.*

*Above: The boiler suit solves the dressing-up
problem beautifully. In white cotton it looks great
with a lithe figure and healthy skin. For parties, in
slippery, colourful fabrics it strikes just the right
casual note.*

FASHIONSTYLES

She takes her dance or exercise kit seriously. It must look good and feel comfortable.

Right: Her favourite skirt is short and slim in denim or tough cotton which she will wear with a crisp shirt, snappy jacket and flat sporty shoes.

A strong sense of physical fitness is vital to Action girl's well-being. She may achieve this by being an enthusiastic games player who is a bonus on the squash or tennis court, a golfer with an admirable handicap or a demon on the hockey pitch. But she is just as likely to prefer her exercise to be of the non-competitive kind. She'll keep her fitness rating up by dance or exercise classes, by regular swimming or jogging sessions, by cycling to work or spending her holidays on the ski slopes. Above all she is the girl who would far rather spend her Sunday afternoon taking a brisk country walk than watching the weekend weepie on T.V.

Obviously she likes her clothes to reinforce her energetic approach to her lifestyle. She wants her clothes to move well, to be fresh and crisp and cleanly cut. She is happiest in sporty separates, with a preppy or collegiate style that is always casual and comfortable. She hates dressing up and has a horror of sophisticated fashion looks. High-heeled shoes are her nightmare, and any hat — except a sporty cap or visor which she loves — makes her feel overdressed and ill-at-ease.

Her first choice for day or evening is trousers. Off duty she will pick easy tracksuits, leggings or ski pants, with shorts the favourite summer alternative. She'll top these with a classic Lacoste short-sleeve sports shirt with the famous crocodile logo; a simple cotton jersey T-shirt or a chunky sweatshirt. She's practical as well as stylish, knotting a plain or cable knit sweater round her neck, all set for a change in temperature while adding to her throwaway style by softening the neckline and bringing in another colour and texture. It's a trick that does the face-framing work of a necklace without the obvious artifice. For less relaxed moments Action girl chooses classic well-cut pleated trousers in good quality fabrics like flannel or gaberdine which she teams with a simple silk or cotton skirt, a golfing cardigan or a cotton rib sweater. Her skirts are short and slim, hovering around the knee, in denim or tough cotton drill — she loves culottes.

Fabric is an important consideration for all her clothes. She chooses the natural fibres that allow her body to breathe freely. The stretch and give of cotton jersey and sweat-shirting or soft wool offer the best option not only for style but also comfort. Her favourite colours are basic blue and white (never black) followed by clear red, royal blue, emerald green and zingy yellow, with pale pink primrose and that peculiar brand of Aertex blue her pastel second string.

Action girl's athletic style of dress has a subtle brand of sex appeal. She may shy away from frilly femininity, vampy glamour or the lady-like classics safe in the knowledge that a lithe body radiating health and dressed in a harmoniously sporty style can prove irresistible.

She wants her clothes to move well, to be fresh and crisp and cleanly cut

Action girl loves to wear updated versions of the sporting classics and borrows freely from traditional sportswear of all kinds for her everyday style of dressing.

Anything with a nautical flavour is spot on for the smart crispness married to practical design that she holds so dear. Naval uniform, whether historical or contemporary, is an endless source of stylish ideas: matelot-stripe sweaters and T-shirts, navy blazers, white sailor pants and broad sailor collars. Modern sailing with its bright primary coloured oilskin jackets, perky caps and Docksider shoes are also beloved of Action girl.

Then there are all the other sports to raid; those tartan Bermuda shorts so favoured by the golfer; the boldly striped shirts of the rugger player; the skier's anorak; the straightforward economy and ease of the racer's swimsuit. These are the kind of clothes that make sense to the girl who wants freedom, not confinement, from fashion.

She appreciates the romantic mood of traditional cricket and tennis clothes before easy-wash synthetic fibres massacred their style. So she will happily wear a pair of baggy cricket flannels teamed with a shirt and chunky cable-knit sweater. Even more flattering with its fluid movement is a long pleated white skirt with V-neck jumper and bright, white canvas shoes.

Paradoxically when Action girl is actually playing tennis − or maybe even cricket in some instances − she chooses the simplest of no-nonsense sports clothes. She may wear a zany head-band but her shirt and brief, pleated skirt or shorts will be of the wash-and-drip-dry variety. She takes her active sports dress seriously, keeping nostalgic sporty styles strictly for everyday.

On shore or afloat, active sports are the inspiration for action clothes

Every sporty style dresser finds the nautical combination of navy and white irresistible. Here a thick navy sweater with a big white cotton picqué sailor collar tops traditional white sailor pants. Perfect kit for an afternoon on the bridge or any inland weekend.

T-shirt dresses are her
best summer stand-by

Action girl will always take the casual way out when a situation demands that she wears something more formal than her favourite shorts and trousers. T-shirt dresses are her best summer stand-by. In supple cotton jersey she buys them in plain bright colours, sometimes spotted or striped or sometimes in bold geometric prints. In winter she simply swops them for a sweater dress which has exactly the same relaxed mood. For extra shape she may belt them loosely round the hips or with an elasticated belt at the waist. She hates feeling restricted and for that reason prefers jackets to coats. Coats flap about the knees while jackets in big baggy blouson styles, easy blazers or hacking jackets leave her free to stride out. Nor need she worry about proportions, as jackets look so much better with trousers.

She is happy when boiler suits and dungarees are in fashion. She will buy them not only for day but for evening too, in soft silk or shiny satin, thereby solving the great problem of what to wear to parties.

You will rarely find her wearing make-up. For a start she doesn't usually need it: her healthy routine and lifestyle give her a clear skin and rosy glow quite naturally. But she's not averse to the lightest dust of blusher, a hint of pink gloss for her lips or a touch of waterproof mascara and neutral eyeshadow when she wants to make an impact. It's never heavy or obvious as this would be totally at odds with her taste in clothes. She keeps her hair simple, either short, well-cut and sporty or in a shoulder-length bob that can easily be tied back.

Left: The easy T-shirt dress in bright yellow cotton jersey that constitutes 'dressing-up' for the action girl.

Right: The casual clothes she loves best: Lacoste shirt teamed with plaid linen Bermuda shorts, sneakers and a sweater tied round her neck.

130

She's a strong swimmer and a dashing diver: you won't catch her wearing a suit that would hamper her performance. Bikinis are not her style. She chooses a one-piece with athletic glamour, high cut sides and a racing back. She'll pick one in a good bright colour or shapely stripes and team it with a racing cap, goggles and a diver's watch.

ACTION GIRL Accessories

The accessories that compliment sporty style have to be as simple and as clean-cut as the clothes themselves. It's a look that won't take fussy femininity, trendy costume jewellery or any item that is too sophisticated. The wrong accessories can ruin this look more surely than any other. The rules are to play it down and don't add anything that doesn't have a practical purpose.

SPORTING **P**ARAPHERNALIA
You can have lots of fun with bits and pieces of sporting paraphernalia; the diver's watch or underwater camera; tennis wristbands, the referee's whistle; the racing driver's lap timer, are all items that look good with sporting clothes and amusing when worn out of context.

STICK **W**ITH **F**LATTIES
Getting the shoes right is vital. High heels and sporty style simply do not mix. A mid-heel with a T-shirt or sweater dress can look marvellous. But stick with the flats as an overall rule. In summer canvas sneakers, espadrilles, plimsoll pull-ons come in a mass of colours and patterns. All year round there are the plain flat pumps, loafers and lace-ups in suede and leather that complement trousers, tracksuits and sporty skirts perfectly.

BAGS, **B**IG **AND** **S**MALL
Bags with sporty origins will make the team. Any variation, big or small, or the hunting shoulder bag in canvas or leather is ideal. So too are sailing kit bags, purse bags that slot on to belts, and knapsacks.

FUN **H**ATS
It's only the sporty hats — the baseball, cricket or yatching caps, the visors, headbands and white sports sunhats — that look good with this style. So have fun with those and leave the flower-trimmed straws in the shop.

Wittily identified by Ann Barr and Peter York back in the 'seventies, Sloane style has survived its spell of notoriety. It's a look that's based on the 'What really matters in life' principle, where clothes are practical, prettily feminine, never flashy, occasionally jokey and always utterly British.

On her sturdy bike, she's sensibly clad in a snug Guernsey, topped by a quilted, waterproof gilet with a corded collar. This could look too severe, if it weren't for the white frilly shirt and pretty floral skirt. Up-to-date Gucci logo shoulder-bag (and snaffle shoes) have the last word.

Above: Puritan collar as a Sloane wears it: very white against a bright blue cardigan, plus the printed swirling skirt.

SLOANE

FASHIONSTYLES

Vital kit for the rural Sloane. The essential Barbour and its stable companions, green Hunter wellington boots, practical tweed breeches in camouflage colours, flat cap and fishing bag, looking so much better on a woman than a man – just some of the things that really matter.

Sloane style is rooted in country clothes, traditional classics that are never out of date

Loathe the name – love the clothes. That's the understandable cry from many a girl whose taste and dress sense has been typecast Sloane but who is far from being a Hooray Henrietta. Forget the ridiculous social implications: concentrate on 'what really matters' – you. You're a traditionalist whose roots are in the country. You hate vulgarity, value femininity and appreciate solid quality. You're a sport with a strong sense of fair play. You enjoy a good joke, love animals, can't be bothered with nail polish except on toes in summer. You ignore fashion, unless it's nostalgic or funny You'll spend money on a good coat, but you're a bargain hunter at heart. Marks and Spencer is the only place you'll buy your undies. You prefer bright, primary colours or dark blues, browns and greens to black (too severe) and pastels (too wishy-washy). You've a keen eye for the right labels – not the high fashion names, but those established firms where the product has been tried and tested for at least one generation. If most of these descriptions can be applied to you, there's little doubt that you are fundamentally inclined towards the style of the Sloane.

Sloanes have come some, if not a long way, since they were first pigeon-holed. The more obvious idiosyncrasies, such as the scarf knotted and balanced precariously on the chin, have been shelved, for the present at least, while other trademarks like navy-blue tights, knickerbockers, velvet for evening and cord for day, have become classic elements in the wardrobe. The urban Sloane, perhaps feeling too conspicuous, has packed up her Husky and sent it out of town, while her country-dwelling sister has multiplied at a truly earthy rate. Any class distinction inherent in Sloane dress has been given the old-heave-ho as Sloane style has become a rural uniform.

Sensible outer layers are vital. Classic coats such as a traditional Austrian loden with the inverted back pleat or a navy wool double-breasted school style with a velvet collar are right on target. Furs and trenchcoats, however, miss by miles, the one too flashy and the other far too smooth. Hallmark of any Sloane worthy of the name is the weatherproof jacket, preferably a genuine Husky or Barbour in hunting green or navy blue. Both the quilted nylon Husky and the oiled cotton Barbour have spawned a host of imitations, but fakes are frowned upon. For Sloane ladies, it must be the real thing.

Sloanes live in separates, with dresses strictly for formal best. Comfort is essential and layer dressing gives room both for manoeuvre and extra warmth. Anything figure hugging or constricting is out – except for trousers, jeans in particular, where the second-skin style is more or less obligatory. Skirts, however, always leave lots of room to move, whether it's a simply gathered dirndl or kilt, pleated or flared. The right fabrics are a vital part of the look. Dirndl or gathered skirts look perfect winter or summer in small, tasteful floral prints on cotton or fine wool, nothing too splashy or bold. Tweed, tartan and cord are favourites for both trousers and skirts.

On top goes a sweater – another Sloane passion. It can be a classic, plain coloured lambswool, Shetland or super luxurious cashmere, long sleeved or sleeveless, and ideally with a crew neck. Both the traditional Aran or Guernsey fisherman's sweater are well-loved, but most highly treasured is the patterned Fair Isle and the hand-knit picture sweater. The Princess of Wales, when an instantly recognizable Sloane in her days as Lady Diana Spencer, wore the now famous red and white sheep jumper with its one black sheep hovering near the left elbow. Sloanes love 'a jolly sartorial jape'. Rarely is the sweater worn next to the skin, for not only would it itch, but would usually mean revealing a naked neck. Sloanes are not fond of nude necks, preferring to be covered by a scarf in winter or better still, to seize the opportunity of wearing a feminine shirt, whether frilly and white, a trad check or even a crisp stripe. While valuing truly feminine touches, the Sloane fully appreciates that clothes borrowed from the boys can often look quite appealing – not, of course, overtly sexy. So – apart from the unisex jackets – she's a great fan of Viyella shirts, flat tweed caps, men's socks and cord breeches – all very hardy and out-door.

TOWN AND GOWN

Left: The sailor dress with a crisp white collar and softening bow is a perennial Sloane favourite. Traditional and gamin, it always looks pretty.

Right: The Loden coat, accessorized with Hermes scarf and Gucci loafers.

Inset: The ball-gown in shocking pink taffeta with flamboyantly décolleté neckline and puff sleeves – it's the one time modesty is dismissed.

Quiet good taste rules the dressed-up daytime Sloane, but at night, for the grand and formal function, she lets rip

138

Dresses that appeal to the Sloane always have a neat, crisp and girlish air. The drop-waisted dress is the most favourite style, partly because it prevents the skinny girl from appearing stick-like and hides a tummy bulge or two on her plumper cousin. Girls who like Sloane style tend to be either naturally skinny or somewhat plump. Hopeless at dieting, they learn to live with their given shape. In cord, wool or velvet in winter and plain red, white or blue cotton gaberdine for summer, with pure white sailor collars for a nostalgic touch, they look enchanting.

When it comes to really dressing up, Sloanes have a well-developed sense of the theatrical. They will own at least one full-length ball dress, probably in a brilliantly coloured crunchy taffeta. Taffeta is the number one fabric because it has enough body to maintain flamboyantly puffed sleeves and luxuriously full romantic skirts, and because it holds colours like Schiaparelli pink, cobalt blue and sizzling scarlet so vividly. The grand ball is the one occasion when a Sloane is happy to throw modesty to the winds − her ball-dress is likely to be décolleté in the extreme. It is, of course, historically quite acceptable to reveal an almost indecent amount of cleavage at a truly formal affair. With the ball-gown will go the best 'real' jewellery she owns. If she's lucky it may be a multi-stranded pearl choker she wears fastened at the front with a large jewelled clasp, plus some suitably flamboyant pearl or diamond earrings − at poorest it will be a simple gold chain around the neck and pearl studs. Bracelets are simply too much.

For less formal functions the Sloane-style dresser still likes colour. Primary silk shirts teamed with matching velvet trousers are a festive stand-by. A velvet suit, the jacket curvy in shape, with military frogging and long sleeves puffed at the shoulder, over a dirndl-shaped skirt is another wardrobe must. It can cope with the cocktail party that is something of an unknown quantity, it's perfect for a winter wedding or even, if differently accessorized, suitable for a funeral. The little black dress, however, has never been an idea that Sloanes feel comfortable with − it's too severe, too understated.

SLOANE Accessories

SLOANES ADORE BOWS

Pretty printed floppy bows tied at the neck of a shirt; sporty men's bow ties; big velvet bows pinned in the hair, all these contribute the romantic touch for which a Sloane strives. A velvet head-band keeps the almost obligatory long hair tidily off the face.

THE REAL THING

There are two ways that Sloanes view jewellery — it must either be the 'real thing' or a witty joke. In the 'real thing' category pearls are far and away the favourites for both day and evening. Pearl earrings — drop or stud — are a must, a string of pearls an investment and a pearl choker a dream.

Timeless classics sum up the Sloane approach to accessories. Never ostentatious, they rely on quiet good taste for their impact. Heaven help the girl who fails to invest in a decent leather shoulder-bag or a classically styled low-heeled pair of pumps. Nor would any Sloane be without her velvet head-band, her pearl earrings, or her Hermès scarf. While these are the essential symbols of the style, the light-hearted touch is equally characteristic, as in amusing pieces of jewellery.

ALL IN A NAME

Sloanes take their shoes and bags very seriously. This is an area in which established labels, standing for high quality of materials and workmanship, count for much. Bags are invariably shoulder-bags, never clutch. Shoes are never stilettos but flat loafers or pumps, rising to mid-heeled courts for dressier occasions. Gilt snaffles and grosgrain bows are pretty and acceptable trimmings.

BUZZ BUZZ

Jewellery jokes are a Sloane foible. They love glittering bug pins, jolly earrings and Mickey Mouse watches.

140

Instant recognition for the now famous sweater worn by the Princess of Wales, in her days as Lady Diana Spencer. Sloanes love hand-knit picture sweaters, especially if they are humorous.

NEW BEATNIK

The New Beatnik Girl feels young and loves fun. Her spirit is pure 'eighties – happy and carefree, confident and brave. Yet she looks to the 'fifties for her inspiration ('cool' jazz is her passion) and to the Beat Generation for her style.

A staple of her wardrobe is her 'sloppy joe' – a huge, capacious sweater like this hand-knitted 'carpet style' one.

Above: Beatnik Girl may team her sloppy joe with ski pants and sturdy lace-up shoes, or wear it on its own as a mini dress with graphically patterned tights, pumps, or the same clompy shoes.

FASHIONSTYLES

For all her youth here's a girl who's sensible too

The new beatnik girl's style is young, sharp and always comfortable. For all her youth, here's a girl who's sensible too. No need to nag *her* to wear an extra hat or scarf if it's cold – for she'll always be prepared. The new beatnik loves to wrap up in her comfy toggled and hooded duffle coat – it speaks 'beat' as clearly as her beret (or her boyfriend's goatee).

The Beatnik Generation emerged in the mid-fifties in the USA. Beatniks were young and 'rad' (radical). They hated squares – anyone who wasn't 'hep', 'cool' or a 'cat'. Beatniks spoke in their own argot which they picked up from jazz musicians and street gangs – one favourite sentence being 'do you dig?' (meaning do you know and like what I mean?). Slaves to jazz music, their heroes were Miles Davis on horn and pianist Thelonious Monk. If there's one

word that sums up all that was sacred to the beatniks – in music as well as attitudes to life – it would be 'cool'. The Beatnik's bible was Jack Kerouac's *On the Road,* a semi-autobiographical novel in which the hero criss-crosses the USA – travelling the road, chasing dreams and jazz music and, more often than not, girls.

The new beatnik girl immerses herself in the words and music of those days. Yet she does not choose to emulate the original lifestyle down to the last detail. She picks out ideas she likes and rejects those that she doesn't. Berets, black polo necks and jazz music all score high on the list of do's. But in the wiser 'eighties, nomad lifestyles, drug addiction and doubtful morals are distinctly unhip.

Very together, new beatnik girl knows her priorities and her style and always gets them right.

A beatnik girl is never without her basic black polo neck sweater, the starting point on which she builds her look. On a cold and windy day she might team it with ski pants, a pinstriped shirt unbuttoned casually and knotted at the waist, and her faithful duffle coat thrown on top. To give the polo-neck sweater a smoother look, she'll button up the shirt and partner it with a snappy straight skirt, opaque black tights and shiny pumps.

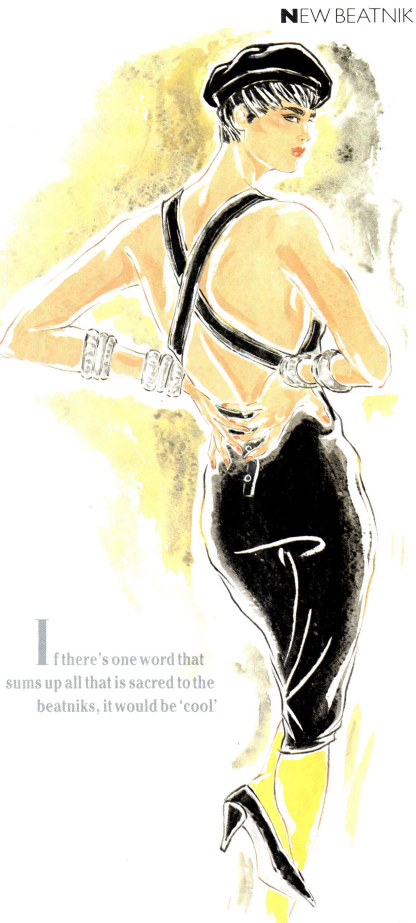

Young and carefree she may be, but come night time Ms Beatnik is the epitome of youthful sophistication. An habituée of hip brasseries and jazz nighteries, her image has got to be cooler than cool. The beatnik girl owns an array of chic little dresses – all of them black, plain and simple. They are skinny little numbers called 'shifts' or 'tubes' in wool jersey, silk or velvet. A strong believer in minimalism and functionalism, she only wears what she needs; 'less is better' – that's her motto. At night time a little black dress is the primed canvas on to which she carefully paints her picture – using the fewest possible accessories with the aim of maintaining chic understatement. At most, she might drape some gilt rope chains about her neck and cram some bangles up her arms. Her dress will remain unadorned, revelling in its pure simplicity. But day or night, the new beatnik girl is never without her trademark – huge hoop earrings.

Preferring simple but dramatic make-up, a night out means a slick of vivid red lipstick and a stroke of black liner on the upper eyelids. Her hair, as always, will not be teased and coaxed into impossible styles, but tousled and ruffled so that it is naturally soft and feathery looking.

New beatnik girl spends hours getting ready when she's going out and about. She's the girl who takes a bath six hours before her date and still isn't ready when the doorbell chimes. Tiny details are of vital importance to this youthful sprite. Her finger and toe nails are manicured to perfection, the finishing touch a coat of pale or clear polish.

Once out, tapping her feet to the driving rhythm of Art Blakey and his Jazz Messengers or listening to the soaring melodies of saxophonist Courtney Pine, the new beatnik girl will look the picture of cool sophistication, confident of her sharp shooting style.

Whether in a night club or brasserie, New Beatnik girl prides herself on her perfectly turned-out appearance. This is what draws her irresistibly to the designs of Azzedine Alaïa.

Left: Alaïa's garments are beautifully cut and shapely, exemplified here by a leather skirt and bodysuit.

Right: This sensuous black dress skims the body and emphasizes her young, sophisticated style.

If there's one word that sums up all that is sacred to the beatniks, it would be 'cool'

147

Back in the 'fifties, long nights in a smoky jazz bar made it relatively easy to look deathly pale – and probably quite interesting, at least while the lights were dim. But the beatnik of the 'eighties is lively and vivacious by nature – and being energetic is her forte. In order to achieve the pale and interesting look to which she aspires, the new Beatnik lets her clothes do the talking, playing up the sought-after sweet fragility of her image. Cleverly she'll shroud herself in a huge cardigan, sweater or coat and more often than not will clutch it to her, immediately giving the impression that she is small and frail. This is a game that new beatnik girl loves to play. For a double life is so exciting. Friends and colleagues are inevitably astounded when they discover how strong and active this girl really is. With a thoroughly 'eighties attitude towards exercise, she loves to run, jump and dance and lifts weights at the gym twice a week.

Looking for all the world like an emigrée from the Left Bank, the modern beatnik girl skilfully combines her love for all things Beat with that for all things French – and brings it off brilliantly, homing in on the points at which the Left Bank and Beatnik looks fuse and interlock. Both styles are known for berets, stripes (black and white or navy and white) and black polo necks. But, most importantly, both are unmistakeably 'cool'.

If she's got the time and the money (our girl always has the inclination) new beatnik girl will head to Paris for a long weekend. Here she'll take a trip on the Bateaux Bouches, and pace her favourite streets in the Latin Quarter on the left bank of the Seine. At a pavement table in a little café, new beatnik girl watches the world pass by, utterly in her element.

The new beatnik girl travels light. She has a compact wardrobe that works well when she's on the move. All that she owns interrelates. She can wear everything with anything and anything with everything. As most of her clothes are black and white, it's not hard for her to mix, match and move around. A beatnik's basic wardrobe consists of six essential pieces: ski pants; a black polo neck; a huge cotton shirt to knot and tie; a straight knee-length skirt; a plain black dress and a capacious sloppy joe. This is her uniform, and with it, new beatnik girl can do no wrong.

As most of her clothes are black and white, it's not hard for her to mix, match and move around

New Beatnik girl's hippest colour has got to be yellow, and yellow worn with black is the ultimate colour combination.

Left: A sleeveless polo neck is matched with stripey jersey leggings and teamed with a huge black mohair cardigan she might have knitted herself. Worn with her trusty Doc Marten-soled shoes, *the New Beatnik girl cuts a striking figure on any land or seascape.*

Above: New beatnik meets Left Bank in a sharp leather suit with a cropped bomber jacket and mini skirt, worn with a neat black and white striped cotton jersey top. With black leather gloves, a black beret and the ubiquitous polo neck the effect is cool and chic.

NEW BEATNIK Accessories

SYMBOLS OF STYLE

A good wool or leather beret — the hat that symbolises beatnik style — is a must in any beat girl's wardrobe — it's comfortable, casual, and can adapt itself to being dressed up or down. The way it is worn is of great significance — pulled down over the forehead and tilted to one side. The beret looks equally good with sweater and skipants by day or with a slinky black dress and high heels by night.

STRIPES, SPOTS AND DOTS

Choosing shoes, the new beatnik girl prefers flats for everyday wear. High heels come out for special occasions, but it's easier to run, jump and dance in a pair of natty black pumps. Coloured and patterned tights are a beatnik girl's penchant . . . she loves geometric stripes, spots and dots in a riotous colour or her favourite graphic black and white.

STYLISH PRACTICALITY

The new beatnik girl chooses her accessories with customary care. A big bag scores high on her list of priorities; made of soft leather, it's easy to open and throw in her essentials — her latest favourite book, mirrored sunglasses, lipstick and keys.

When choosing a belt, beatnik girl always makes sure she owns a real waist cincher — great for transforming that roomy sweater dress into something shapely. Our beatnik girl loves silver, like the hoop earrings and bangles at the heart of her jewellery collection.

New beatnik girl would describe her style as 'functional minimalism'. Clean cuts and simple lines are of vital importance to her — the ultimate expression of what she most admires would be a model of understatement — a black bodysuit which she could wear on its own, or with her ski pants or with a short snappy, straight skirt.

Left: Black knit bodysuit clings and flatters, while allowing sweet freedom of movement, looking up-to-the-minute with strikingly spotted tights.

CLASSIC

The woman who wears the classic style never puts a foot wrong. Everything about her is elegant, cool and expensive. She can outshine every other woman in the room, and yet afterwards you may not be able to remember *exactly* what she was wearing.

The trenchcoat is a must, now stylishly reinterpreted for the 'eighties. The classic kilt in white fine wool and simple silk shirt are quietly accessorized with grey and brown leather bag and beautifully crafted shoes.

Above: International classic, bringing an essentially female flair to the familiar blazer, 501 jeans, man's shirt and cowboy belt.

The woman who appreciates the classic is something of a perfectionist. A classic earns its name because of its faultless design. It endures, decade after decade, because it was so good in the first place: well cut, beautifully put together, entirely simple. With her well-trained eye, the classic dresser sees and appreciates the qualities that have enabled a classic to last the course, and can disregard what is no more than fashionable, tawdry and vulgar. She has no 'mistakes' lurking in the back of her wardrobe. What she buys today she is fully confident she will be wearing in ten years' time, with perhaps only discreet modification: a little extra padding at the shoulder, a complete switch of accessories. The classic dresser with style treads a fine line. She never looks dated, without ever looking foolishly trendy.

The rules for successful classic style are few: only the best fabrics; neutral colours lifted by the subtlest, classiest pastels; classic shapes by established names; expensive, quality accessories. A slavish adherence to these rules, however, results in a dull imitation of the real thing – the appearance of taste without the back-up of discernment. The classic dresser's cousin never breaks a rule, but you would not notice her in a room. The classic dresser with style, however, always stands out; her clever juxtaposition of cool and dark neutrals give a vibrant effect without the use of bright colour.

This is not a young girl's look, and because the classic dresser is entirely confident in her quintessential womanhood, she can wear the simple, sometimes severe, occasionally masculine, lines of her style while still exuding femininity and an utterly discreet sexiness. That is why, at her most casual, she can wear with panache the jeans and blazer look. The jeans, of course, must be Levi Strauss' 501s. That opportunistic entrepreneur who took bales of cloth to make into tents for the miners in the Californian goldrush showed indomitable optimism when he arrived and found they had tents galore. He simply turned his serge de Nimes into trousers cut like those worn by Genoese sailors. These 'denim' 'jeans', perfectly cut, indestructible, practical, are the obvious choice for a classic dresser, who sees no point in buying a high street copy when the originals are still available.

But what distinguishes the fashion-conscious classic dresser from her purely traditional counterpart is knowing instinctively when it is possible to depart from the original. The Burberry trenchcoat is a case in point. Everyone appreciates the quality of this khaki mac, actually for use in the trenches, with its impenetrable weatherproofing and utterly practical details. But the fashion-conscious classicist, confident in her sense of style, happily opts for an updated version, a model with all the inherent qualities of the original and no less expensive – but with the stylish details she prefers.

Evening sees her very simply dressed. She prefers the kind of clothes that rely on clever cutting: nothing revealing or overtly sexy, but always feminine. She will wear black or navy or true, clear colours – never ornate prints or pretty-pretty frills. Proportions are important. She will choose a stunning little jacket where a coat could spoil the line of her dress. It could be of oriental design, a short fur, or the softest suede in a vivid shade.

Everything is a little more emphatic in the evening. Her make-up is bolder, her jewellery more impressive

Right: A deceptively simple turquoise suede jacket, smooth as swansdown and softly gathered at the shoulder.

Left: The navy silk evening dress, a masterpiece of clever cutting.

The classic dresser is not a clothes horse, drawing attention to her wonderful outfit

Right: The twinset updated, now with a polo-player's shirt collar and trio of buttons. In primrose cotton, its pedigree is evident in deep ribbing to wrist and waist, sitting comfortably over pleat-fronted grey trousers.

Left: Chanel lives on re-interpreted for the 'eighties by Karl Lagerfeld. The ultimate in chic, every detail is correct, on the collarless jacket with its patch pockets, braid and buttons and on the sinuous wrap-around skirt.

Grace Kelly is perhaps the epitome of the classic style, cool and classy. Whatever she wore, *she* looked wonderful – not simply the clothes. For the classic dresser is not a clothes horse, drawing attention to her wonderful outfit. She is signalling, 'I have *very* good taste', to people in the know.

As with every look, there are the clichés – in this case it is 'twinset and pearls'. But the clever classic dresser is too stylish to wear anything that could be lightly dismissed. Her twinset has evolved: looser without being baggy, and in a rich creamy shade with a texture to match. Touch the

sleeve of this cardigan and your fingers won't rasp on coarse lambswool or shetland. She will be wearing a silky cotton knit or cashmere; even if the texture is interestingly rustic or uneven, it will not be harsh.

She frequently wears trousers; usually the traditional pleat-fronted straight-legged style. But she makes some concessions to fashion. If jodhpurs are 'in', she will wear them: but not a designer copy – the real thing. In the same way, you might see her striding out in corded landgirl trousers (not a fashion invention in gaberdine) if the situation demanded it.

A hidden bonus of classic dressing is that the shape, cut and fabric are immensely flattering to the figure. No woman with the discipline to master classic dressing would be lazily fat, but under those fluid lines could lurk the famous English pear shape.

The classic dresser may not be born rich, but she is prepared to save for individual items of great quality. She will not buy much, but what she buys lasts. If money only marries money, then the poor-little-rich-girl classic dresser with her elegant air has the best chance of marrying into wealth of anyone.

157

Just because something cost a fortune doesn't mean it must be treated with reverence

The perfectionist does not relax her standards when off duty. Style goes all the way through her, and is usually inborn. She never slouches or slumps, but drapes, and does not seem different when she is casual, because she is *always* casual. Just because something cost a fortune doesn't mean it must be treated with reverence. Indeed, part of the style is nonchalance. Having put her look together with infinite care, she then forgets about it, as if it were supremely unimportant. Throughbred elegance cannot be caught off-guard. Those who attempt to copy her sometimes get it wrong because they are over-contrived. She never co-ordinates too strictly. Matching top, skirt, handbag and shoes can be desperately dowdy, whatever the quality.

There'd be something almost prudish about her underwear, if it weren't for the slippery, sensuous texture of the fabric — pure silk. She wouldn't wear an uplift, under-wired bra. She is practical enough always to wear a petticoat, even though her skirts are lined, to add extra fluidity to the movement of her clothes.

There is an element of snobbery about the classic look. You have to be in the know to know: one line of detail stitching is right on a particular garment, whereas two is possibly − just − over the top. On something else the double row could be crucial. Some of the items that go to make up a classic wardrobe, such as the 501s, have become highly prized because they are the very best of their kind.

Many of them are English, dating from the days when quality was the hallmark of English workmanship. European neighbours are willing to travel to acquire them, which is what gives even the essentially English items a peculiarly European jet-set look.

Her sisters everywhere all prefer expensive-looking colours: black and white, camels and costly pastels; neutrals, such as brown, grey and navy − never the bright primaries or anything remotely startling.

This classic dresser keeps her chic right through till bedtime. Not for her a lacy-trimmed negligée and nightie set, but a soft cashmere man's dressing down in darkest navy blue, over oyster pink satin pyjamas.

Above: Pure perfection in dress extends to underwear too: shell pink camisole and French knickers, pearly grey petticoat.

159

CLASSIC Accessories

THE PERFECT BAG
Originally designed for Grace Kelly, the rectangular Kelly bag of tan leather, closed with padlock and key, is a great day-time accessory, matched to wrist-length gloves and wide belt.

ONLY THE BEST
More than any other accessory, the right choice of jewellery reflects the sureness of touch of its wearer: on one wrist a gold bangle, on the other a Cartier watch; an important buckle of silver on a leather belt, and Russian rings of inter-woven white, red and yellow gold.

QUALITY FOOTWEAR
Perfection top-to-toe means superb quality footwear, whether riding boots so beautifully made and from such gleaming leather that they need no ornament; Italian court shoes for the ultimate in simple elegance or low heeled two-tone lace-ups, the last word in comfort.

Accessories make or mar the classic style, and it is particularly important to get the jewellery absolutely right, with Chanel-made or Chanel-inspired costume jewellery, for example, bold and brilliant, but never vulgar. She chooses only simple shoes and bags, usually Italian, of the finest leather. Labels are very important: if you can't afford a Cartier Santos watch, go without – a copy could ruin everything.

CLASSIC SHADES
Jackie Onassis made the look her own, leaving her signature in dark glasses and gold hoop earrings, enduring components in the classic collection.

Whether she wears her hair
tousled or sleek, the cut is
impeccable. Skin-care is just
as important as make-up,
which is flawless:
monochromatic eye make-up,
a touch of mascara, and
creamy rose-coloured lips.
Her face is framed by
jewellery from Chanel,
gleaming audaciously at ears
and throat.

JETSETTER

You can spot her at any international airport, the jet-set girl who knows how to travel and arrive in style. Her long hair, chic luggage and slick relaxed look of understated glamour are an instant give-away.

Teamed with baggy white Capri pants, bold jewellery and a hat, the velvet top of a shapely black swimsuit guarantees maximum poolside allure and attention.

Above: The stunning black velvet swimsuit which doubles up as a dramatic top and scores high for chic on its own

Whether she is off to walk in the Himalayan foothills or to soak up some sun and social fun at the St James Club, Antigua, the jet-set girl has her clothes packing perfectly judged. She is our alter-ego, the girl we all wish to emulate on our own perhaps less exotic trips to a fortnight of fun in Frinton or a long anticipated package deal to some Mediterranean beach resort.

The jet-set girl knows how to dress to beat the crumple and crease of the weary traveller. She knows exactly what the sartorial demands will be when she reaches her destination. She keeps her basic clothes simple, sticking to the tried and tested sun-proved stunners, which can be accessorized in her own confident and dramatic style.

Her daytime clothes consist of little more than a wonderful collection of bikinis and swimsuits, all linked to clever cover-ups of the informally glamorous type. She may wear a large sun-hat, big sunglasses and carry a capacious straw bag but she won't look over-dressed. Her style is laid-back.

At night the jet-set girl gets dressed up. Her look is international with the emphasis on simply cut sexy clothes. She loves slinky, silky cutaway vest tops to wear with a short, wrap sarong skirt or baggy pyjama pants. She is never without a black or white strappy or halter neck sundress in soft silk or jersey which will skim and cling and reveal her tan to perfection. She wears bustier or bandeau tops with tight leggings or baggy shorts, accessorized after sunset with bold modern jewellery or a profusion of ethnic pieces collected on her travels.

Jet-set girl is never without a tan. She doesn't precisely ignore the warnings of the harmful and ageing effects of excess sun, but she would hate to be aspirin pale. She takes care of her skin, is an expert on the latest and best in sun protection creams but she must be brown.

Left: At night the jet-set girl dresses up international style in slinky black silk jersey vest and wrap sarong skirt.

Below: Safari colours look so good in the heat. Comfortable loose linen dress buttoned through for comfort and versatility, can be accessorized up or down, day or night.

This girl travels light. Her Vuitton suitcase can be relied on to contain everything she needs for her high-style profile, economically

FASHIONSTYLES

On any trip she travels light. Overloaded suitcases cramp her style. Even on a far-flung journey she will take no more than she can carry herself. Porters are a thing of the past. She likes to travel quickly with the minimum of fuss. Knowing that customs will always stop the girl in the fur coat or an obviously ritzy looking rig, she dresses classily but quietly.

Clothes that come in loose, comfortable layers are a priority. Air travel, as any stewardess will tell you, causes the body to swell, just enough to make skimpy or tight clothes unbearable. Layer dressing means you can pile on or peel off, to move from a cool to a hot climate and back again looking and feeling good. No shivering at one destination or sweating profusely at the other.

She starts with a mannishly chic jacket teamed with an easy slim skirt or trousers, picking fabrics that are either designed to look their best marginally crumpled like linen or denim, or those that stay immaculately creaseless in spite of heavy duty wear, like worsted, or gaberdine.

Under a shirt or sweater jet-set girl will put a pristinely white T-shirt — they're her travelling stock in trade. She buys them by the dozen in super quality jersey that washes well to stay looking brand new for longer. Always fresh and simple, that bright white will reflect a flattering light to a face that may be jet-lag pale or perfectly tanned.

In her soft, squashy travel bag, she carries — along with the necessities of life like a good book, make-up and toothbrush — a change of undies for an unscheduled stop-over; a mineral water spray for refreshing dull, dehydrated skin and a pair of socks to keep her feet warm on long-haul flights.

Left: A city destination requires perfectly creaseless chic. Jet-set girl picks a lightweight check wool suit and a crisp white shirt.

Right: Holiday bound, her style relaxes down to a denim suit teamed with her favourite white T-shirt, super star sunglasses and a strongly individual belt.

Above: If there's a chic way of coping with a beauty problem jet-set girl will know what it is. When her long hair's still wet from the sea and needs protection from the fierce sun, she covers it with a filmy printed chiffon scarf, kept firmly in place with a crownless hat.

Jet-set girl has an encyclopedic knowledge of the world. She's the one who holidayed last year in the spot everyone else seems to be visiting this year. She knows the best — though not necessarily the biggest — hotels in any place you care to mention. Her knowledge may not always be first-hand, but she always has a very good friend tucked up her sleeve who has been going there for years. She's the girl you can rely on to pick out the best night-clubs and the trendiest restaurants; she knows not only the First Secretary at the Embassy who will work miracles when your passport and purse have been stolen, but also a local dressmaker who can whip up copies of the chicest silk shirt overnight. She understands fashion on an international level. Her clothes are slick and sexy, though not always wildly expensive. While she will flirt with the latest silly craze currently promenading the beaches of St Tropez or gracing the clubs and cafés of the Riviera, nevertheless she appreciates the impact to be made by stunning simplicity worn with dash and style. She has the gift of knowing how to make heads turn.

Beaches and swimming pools loom large in a jet-setter's lifestyle. Her swimsuit collection is enormous and often startlingly original. She will own a one-piece that is the acme of current fashion, something bold, amusing and probably quite outrageous. But the mainstay of her swimsuit range will be the deceptively simple suits and bikinis that look nothing off but a million dollars on. They're beautifully cut, invariably expensive and usually black. For topless sunbathing she wears a miniscule thong that fits and flatters to perfection. If she has to be more modestly dressed — though she would

prefer not — she picks a small strapless bandeau topped bikini which eliminates the marks that mar a perfect tan. An active water sports enthusiast, she will slip into a shapely suit that won't let her down or hamper her in her energetic pursuit.

She pays equal attention to the cover-up she chooses to get her to and from the beach. Again, glamour is a vital consideration. You won't catch her scrambling out of a full complement of clothes on the sand or struggling back into them when it's time for a lobster and spritzer lunch. Her favourite cover-up is an African kanga, one of those long, simple rectangular lengths of fabric which are often brightly coloured or boldly printed. She cleverly wraps, tucks and ties her kanga into a dress, a playsuit or a skirt, swiftly and deftly in a matter of seconds. In cooler climes she may throw a super-soft towelling robe around her shoulders. She is not the kind of girl who buys elaborate beach 'sets', as her aim is to look relaxed — not contrived or over co-ordinated.

Jet-set girl knows how to get the best out of colour. Black and white may be the basic neutrals of her wardrobe, but she would never ignore the power of the primaries when it comes to making an impact. She has a stock of silky T-shirts and skimpy vests in a mass of different shades that she will team with crisp white trousers and, of course, shorts. This girl loves shorts of all descriptions, from baggy Bermudas to pedal pushers that fit like a second skin, from tight short shorts to loose, prettily printed boxer-style numbers. In the heat, shorts are easy and cool to wear, and look as much at home on the deck of an up-market yacht as they do on a visit to a local bazaar.

Jet-set girl knows how to get the best out of colour . . . she would never ignore the power of the primaries when it comes to making an impact

Right: These prettily printed shorts feel comfortable and look great in the heat of the day, combining well with any number of plain skimpy tops.

JETSETTER

Accessories

EXOTIC ARTS

Headscarves are the easiest way to cover up hair that needs protection from the sun. Jet-setter has mastered the art of weaving two or three into an exotic and extremely flattering turban. Cotton is better than silk as it doesn't slip about or slide off. Brilliant hues of citrus and blossom are repeated in a tanned armful of bangles. All jewellery, like the enormous hoop earrings, is bold and modern, simple and eye-catching. Dramatic without being ostentatious, with props like these it's the work of a moment to switch from lazing by the pool to sipping piña colada at the bar. Vivid lipstick and matching fingernails, always immaculately applied, provide the finishing touches to this glamorous look.

RING THE CHANGES

Beautifully cut, cool and comfortable white shorts accentuate a shapely waist, when belted up with a slim strap of cerise, a bright green buckle at the centre. Belts in each one of the tropical shades that highlight this tightly knit collection quickly make casual clothes more formal and draw attention to the body they encircle.

Like stylish ladies of whatever persuasion, jet-setter makes her accessories justify their place. In the interests of travelling light, she chooses a soft squashy bag that stays with her in flight. Inside await the bangles, scarves and little strappy tops that work wonders with her streamlined collection of basics.

Opposite: A luxurious robe of hot orange towelling bound in cool blue doubles up as day-time cover over a toning one-piece swimsuit with flatteringly high-cut legs.

LOCAL COLOUR

The bazaar's the place to find a huge straw basket, the only way to deal with beach paraphernalia. A hat's indispensable, the largest to be found for maximum impact and coverage. Straw belts are cool, pretty (and cheap), while very simple sandals are the next best thing to bare feet.

Despite the romance in her name, Second-hand Rose has a determined mind and a sharp eye for cost-effective ways to achieve designer looks. With second-hand and surplus clothes at the heart of her wardrobe, she re-interprets the looks of yesteryear with stunning results.

SECOND-HAND ROSE

An Australian army jacket from the local surplus store is tightly buttoned and belted over a slim, wrap-over skirt, a silhouette fit for the parade. Rose makes it special with a wayward hat, loads of beads and 'twenties shoes.

Above: Enhance the military air with brass or gold buttons. The same jacket slips over a perfectly plain sweater and cuts a dash with jodhpurs from the surplus store.

FASHIONSTYLES

Don't be fooled by the title. This Second-hand Rose is emphatically '86. She would rather wither and die than be considered dowdy, down-at-heel or – God forbid – dated! This girl's style is inspired. How *does* she do it?

Second-hand Rose knows fashion inside out. She reads the best up-market womenswear glossies as well as the more avant-garde style bibles, and is forever one hundred per cent au fait with the hottest designer names, from Katherine Hamnett to Azzedine Alaïa, even though she doesn't own a stitch of their costly clothing. Undaunted by the restrictions of her budget (she spends money on shelter, study and survival) her innate flair for contemporary style enables her to interpret each season's mood on a shoestring, employing boundless ingenuity. She can wander along the most fashionable shopping streets looking entirely at home among some very expensive creations. Everything about her looks right. Her hair is precision cut, glossy and sculptured into the season's favourite shape. Her light make-up has been faultlessly applied and she sports only the latest colours. Her clothes are simply, perfect. Flat pumps, fashionably rumpled stockings, feminine frock coat and that skirt! – You just have to ask, where did she buy it? Only to be told 'Oh, in some old junk shop, can't remember where – only cost me a pound. A real find'.

Ouch. You have just met second-hand Rose. Her vague answer was, in fact, highly characteristic. This girl has many secrets. She enjoys working hard to achieve that enviable result, but couldn't bear to feel anyone even realized she was trying!

Rose is confident in the knowledge that it is almost impossible for contemporary designers to be totally original, and that many styles come and go in cycles. She has made it her business to discover a handful of second-hand shops where her expert eye recognizes suitable shapes, colours and fabrics which can be used to create the season's look. Rose knows more: some retro clothing is finished to a delightfully high standard. Cotton and suiting react well to minor repairs or even major alterations while both cotton and silk absorb dyes particularly well. A modern city dweller, Rose travels out of town to scour the jumble sales. She knows that older, more established communities tend to discard better quality clothing while city sales tend to be filled with worn-out, undesirable man made fibres which don't wear or look particularly good. Our girl is acutely aware of quality and is always on the look-out for the best natural fabrics – pure wool handknits, wool crepe suits, tweed coats, gaberdine raincoats, mens suiting and crisp, cotton shirts, bright woven cotton skirts and seductive swathes of silk and lace lingerie; these are a few of her favourite things.

Rose is also switched on to the visual power of clever accessorizing which can give the most simple outfit a neat, contemporary twist. Her wardrobe boasts a colourful array of second-hand hats, gloves, shoes, scarves and jewellery – all inexpensively bought and lovingly cared for. Having set aside diary dates for her jumble sales excursions and ensured that the lady in the second-hand shop is on the lookout for that pinstripe fabric she needs, Rose makes her way to the local surplus store. Not that she would ever appear looking like an obvious uniformed stereotype. But she knows that military basics are made to last, fashioned out of resilient fabrics which, with a little imagination, can be put to a hundred different uses.

Her innovative streak enables her to take a strict, tailored jacket and wear it out of context over a soft, print dress – or give a neat RAF wool skirt a touch of femininity teamed with a shapely sweater, some understated jewellery and flattering pumps. For summer, military 'white' – particularly cropped, waiter-style jackets, and roomy cotton drill pants are a terrific buy. Rose also keeps her eagle eye open for dressy buttons or emblems with which to transform plain coats and jackets. Surplus stores are also a useful source of the type of regulation men's underwear – T-shirts, leggings and vests – which dye beautifully to become endlessly versatile summer outerwear.

Other potentially good surplus buys are riding boots, belts, land army-style breeches, cotton shorts, jodhpurs and thick, black plastic raincoats. For that extra special 'one-off' item – an irresistible silk or satin shift, or an outrageous evening creation, Rose religiously attends the Sunday antique markets – not only are they fun to wander round but oh, the joy of that find!

The style may be nostalgic . . . but the accessorizing must be up-to-the-minute

A swirling floral skirt circa 1950, its fullness used to good effect under a tail coat and teamed with long cotton socks and flat pumps.

Left: A great summer look for now – Rose wears the 'fifties skirt with a shapely blouse and wide white belt.

175

FASHION STYLES

If there's one item in Rose's wardrobe she would never be without it's probably a stone gaberdine raincoat that she discovered on a market stall three years ago and has worn regularly ever since. Apart from the practical plus of being a girl's best friend in British weather, the timeless gaberdine simply has the innate charm of spelling style whenever, however it is worn. Another advantage is that these raincoats are relatively easy to find – grab one at a jumble sale or second-hand shop or borrow one from a boyfriend, brother or father (on a long term basis, of course).

The magic of this garment has been recognized by most top designers and features in almost every ready-to-wear collection season after season. Its most effective champion in Britain is probably Katherine Hamnett. The flattering, yet casual and easycare qualities of the look have become synonymous with the ever-popular Hamnett philosophy of style. Another appealing feature is that almost everyone seems to be able to give this garment their individual hallmark. Wear it belted or unbelted, the belt buckled or casually tied, buttoned or loose, perhaps rolling back the sleeves to reveal a flash of unexpected colour (linings are relatively simple to replace). The style may be nostalgic – Bogart and Bacall – but the accessorizing must be up-to-the minute.

Rose wears her raincoat over a pair of cotton drill side-zipped trousers – a shape very flattering to the female form, with a curvy, deep-revered blouse. The coat looks just as good over a slim skirt and high heels and can be endlessly accessorized. One day Rose will pin a brooch to the lapel, on another knot a silk scarf at the neck or top the ensemble with a rakish trilby or Breton style beret.

Coats are a great second-hand buy. Rose knows that wonderful quality tweed and woollen fabrics are still waiting to be found, even cashmere at marvellous prices. She looks out for swirly, brightly coloured duster shapes which look brilliant teamed with a party dress by night, or easily create a more colourful daytime look.

Whatever the scene, Rose realizes how important it is to mirror her apparel with appropriate hair and make-up. Starting from the top, her hair is cut once a month at a hairdressing school where she offers her services free as a model. It's a mid-length versatile style which she can change to match her mood by utilizing her hoard of accessories – one day a Chanel-type bow, the next a colourful length of fabric wrap, or, the addition of her favourite extra – long pony tail hairpiece.

She keeps her make-up simple but enjoys experimenting to complement an outfit – and of course Rose knows of a very clever popular range which is forever one step ahead with inexpensive, good quality, up-to-the minute colours.

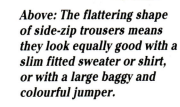

Above: The flattering shape of side-zip trousers means they look equally good with a slim fitted sweater or shirt, or with a large baggy and colourful jumper.

The style may be nostalgic . . . but the accessorizing must be up-to-the-minute

A raincoat or big coat is a must. Its clean lines make it a classic, but it is also versatile, being both practical and stylish. Teamed here with tight trousers, it would look just as good over a long, full skirt. The hairstyle is low-key, the make-up barely there.

177

FASHIONSTYLES

Usually fashioned into suits with tapering trousers or tailored skirts, soft, chalky stripes on black, grey, brown, navy or airforce blue are a perennial daytime favourite. Pinstripe has the quality of making almost anyone who wears it look smart and respectable; hence its association with certain lifestyles. More recently, the stuffier side of the image has thankfully been diminished through an inspired revival of the fabric by a number of leading designers – most notably, Jean-Paul Gaultier – who have cut the cloth on softer lines and exaggerated its proportions, often adding witty, unexpected touches such as a full, colourful net skirt squeezed out of the hem of a tight pinstripe one!

Rose gives pinstripe the new treatment here to create an ultimately feminine, contemporary look. She exaggerates the smartness of the fabric, nipping in the waist of a tailored jacket and using braces to hold up a skirt which certainly would not fall down without them. She is wearing her braces unconventionally crossed – certainly the most comfortable way for a girl.

The long, slim skirt is worn with flat shoes to create the correct proportions. Teamed with a crisp, cotton shirt or a soft polo neck, the overall look makes an understatement no-one can ignore. For a different effect, Rose sometimes adopts a pair of heavy-rimmed glasses (use plain glass if your eyes are O.K.) while emphasizing her femininity with a wittily exaggerated hairdo. Pinstripe dry-cleans well and rarely creases – making it the perfect day-to-night basic. After working late at the office, Rose piles on some chains, applies ruby red lipstick and is instantly out on the town!

Men's pinstripe trousers are simple to alter and look sensational gathered and loosely belted over a plain shirt, worn with a tight waistcoat or oversized jacket and brogues. The coat and trousers of a pinstripe suit don't have to be worn together. Rose often slips her favourite jacket over a simple wool dress, and knows it will look even more stunning with other prints.

Right: A two-piece pinstripe suit – its smartness accentuated with the addition of braces and glasses. The jacket has been taken in at the waist to give a really curvy shape over the long, tight skirt.

A man's pair of pinstripe trousers teamed with a cotton shirt — again the waist is defined by wearing a boned fine-spot waistcoat, and pulled together with a wide belt. Femininity is the keyword — keeping the colours soft while the mood stays strong.

Pinstripe gets a new treatment to create an unstuffy, ultimately feminine, contemporary look

The little black dress, re-interpreted year after year by generations of designers. It's the simplest way to look stunning. Rose adds long gloves and a net hat for that Breakfast at Tiffany's look.

Nighttime, and Rose attracts a great deal of attention in one of the shapely dresses from her collection, many of them crafted in fabrics of rare quality. Rose enjoys the romance of the golden age of the great evening couturiers like Balenciaga, Madame Grès and Givenchy. Now that the shorter, less restricting 'cocktail' length is acceptable almost everywhere, Rose realizes that contemporary designers have drawn heavily from those former masters, making it possible to wear a well-chosen second-hand dress with no fear of looking out-of-date. The 'eighties designers Rose looks to for eveningwear direction are Azzedine Alaïa (body-consciousness), Jasper Conran (languid chic) and the Italian maestro, Giorgio Armani (clean and elegant shapes).

The thrill of hunting for second-hand eveningwear lies in the distinct possibility of finding a meticulously hand-finished garment which would be astronomically priced today. Rose looks out for slim silhouettes and soft, flowing fabrics which drape, swirl or adhere to the body. Clean, uncluttered lines in sumptuous material tend to be the best investment – shapes with maximum sex appeal which can be loaded with accessories but make an equally effective statement worn alone.

Rose searches for diaphanous chiffon, delicate lace, pure silk, wool crepe, velvet and satin for both full-length and evening dresses, and will also be on the alert for some of the spectacular appliqué and beadwork that's still to be found on dresses, bolero jackets and sometimes evening coats. She might even track down heavily beaded dresses from the 'twenties but will check the strength of the beadwork before risking a spirited shimmy. The best potential evening wear buy is that indispensable Little Black Dress which can mean anything from chic restraint to high voltage glamour and always enables the individual to shine through. Rose's personal favourite is inspired by Audrey Hepburn a la *Breakfast at Tiffany's,* jewellery at a minimum, with the simple addition of full-length black gloves and a frothy net hat to set her apart from the crowd. Her make-up is appropriately precise; glossy lipstick and sharp streaks of deftly applied black eyeliner. The alternative is no-holds-barred glamour, embodied in a dress of spectacular colour or cut, which begs for loads of jewellery and vivid makeup.

Second-hand shops are Aladdin's caves for evening accessories – lace or satin gloves, beaded clutch bags, cocktail hats, seamed stockings and piles of diamanté and glass costume jewellery.

The dress is an epitome of the 'fifties, dramatic in colour and daring in cut and detail. Rose wears it with thoroughly modern aplomb and a duster coat draped nonchalantly over one shoulder.

181

It's always worth investing in something which is obviously very special, such as a pink silk 'thirties nightdress – a beautiful item that feels as good as it looks.

SECOND HAND ROSE

Accessories

FINE FEATHERS

The pleasure of antique hats lies half in the terrific impact they have, half in the attention to detail: this head-turning example has a crown of shot silk bound in velvet, the feathers set to tremble at every move of the head.

THE TEST OF TIME

No modern leather briefcase has the appeal of one that's done good service through the years, aged into softness and still with a great future. To further enhance her pinstripe look, Rose seeks — and finds — a sober dotted scarf; silk, of course.

Let others sport their quartz. Rose prefers a no-nonsense timepiece vintage 1930, its sturdy tan strap and clearly visible face betraying its masculine origins. She'll search high and low for just the right tan gloves, cut wrist length so the watch can still be seen.

Like every stylish dresser with her finger on the pulse of fashion, Rose never underestimates the power of accessories. What characterizes her approach is that it is thoroughly eclectic. Whenever she sees a head-turning hat, soft old leather handbag or printed silk shawl, she snaps it up, knowing that it will earn its place in her wardrobe ten times over. Her insistence on top quality (at low prices) makes sure of that.

PLEASURE PRINCIPLE

Rose wouldn't work so hard at finding the right clothes if she didn't enjoy it so much. The final touch that makes you smile is part of her objective. Hence the witty Chanel-type bow, sure to be placed at the neck of a shirt that least expects it; hence the glint in the eye of the cat at her ear, the jangle of junk jewellery, the impossible twist in her hair. And the shoes, with their waisted heel and ankle strap? they're just sexy.

183

LOOKING AFTER YOUR CLOTHES

Taking the time and trouble to look after your clothes halves the eventual effort needed to appear well-groomed. Most of the do's and don't's of clothes care are drummed into us in childhood, the perfectly obvious routines that we don't tend to carry out consistently through tiredness, laziness or a lack of sufficient wardrobe and other storage space. It's tempting, after a long and tiring day, just to throw your clothes over a chair as you take them off – the extra minute to smooth them out and hang them up seems just too much and, of course, they can be pressed and hung up tomorrow. But this is storing up trouble for yourself if it means you have to spend part of your leisure time sorting and ironing clothes unnecessarily, or snatch vital minutes out of another day's preparation.

There are four commonsense rules that bring order to your clothes collection and keep garments in top condition, ready to wear at a moment's notice.

1 Organize your cupboard so that everything has its appointed place – from evening dresses to chunky sweaters, from shoes to scarves. Make sure every item is easy to locate and can be quickly put away.

2 Always hang up clothes while they retain some body heat and creases are likely to fall out rather than multiply. In the same way fold sweaters neatly, smoothing the body and sleeves as you fold.

3 Put dirty clothes that are washable straight into the laundry basket. Clothes that must be dry-cleaned can be hung up separately or put into a bag ready for the trip to the cleaners.

4 Never hang up or fold away anything that needs mending. You'll only forget about it and have a rush repair job on your hands next time you want to wear it.

BASIC CLOTHES CARE EQUIPMENT
Plastic, wood or padded coat-hangers
Clip hangers for trousers and skirts
Travel iron or portable steamer
Clothes brush
Shoe trees
Shoe cleaning kit
Small bedroom sewing kit

LIFESTYLES FASHIONSTYLES

CLOTHES STORAGE

It's one of those unwritten laws that however much space you have to store your clothes, it is never quite enough. But there are many solutions that will ease the problem. Your clothes need to be well-organized and readily visible if you are to get the maximum mileage from them. It's possible to forget the existence of some things if they are buried too deeply in the wrong place.

Start by looking at your wardrobe. In winter, pack away your strictly fair-weather things and vice versa in the summer. Make sure they are properly protected while they are stored. Wrap individual items in tissue or polythene and keep them together in a sturdy box or, better still, in a suitcase which you'll need to store anyway, unless you go away very frequently.

Give the clothes you haven't worn for a season some long hard consideration. Will you ever wear them again? If the answer is no or the chances are slim, be ruthless, send them to the local good cause and utilize the space you've saved. Clothes that are relatively unworn may be saleable in a nearly-new second-hand shop and this could provide a small amount of cash towards something more useful. For Second-hand Roses, a thorough shake-out of your wardrobe provides a good opportunity to bag up the things you've grown tired of and go to your favourite haunts to check out the recently arrived stock. Perhaps you can part-exchange your returns for another unusual bargain.

While you're about it, do a review of your storage space and decide whether you have enough space of the right kind to house your clothes collection. Perhaps the number of items you keep overall has expanded, or you have more things which need to hang rather than fold, as compared to last year's wardrobe. For the clothes fanatic, the ultimate luxury is a large walk-in closet, lit from above and logically divided between hanging space, drawers and shelving. If your wardrobe has outgrown a piece of purpose-built furniture, is there a chance of converting a small utility room or large alcove? It may be worth it if clothes are a

priority in your life. Is overcrowding making your clothes look limp and creased because they haven't room to breathe? Are coats and long dresses hanging clear of the wardrobe base? Not everyone is lucky enough to have room to play with in an apartment or a house, but it's useful to apply some lateral thinking to storage organization when your clothes closet itself becomes the problem.

When creating additional space for clothes which are kept flat or folded, your solution may depend on whether you prefer them concealed or on display. If you can arrange some new shelving it can be fitted with doors or disguised by an attractive curtain or blind over the whole area. If you like your wardrobe available at a glance, there is a good range of open shelving and pull-out racks to choose from. Check out the solutions used in shops and stores, but remember they are dealing with short-term storage for a fast turnover of stock. Plan your own fixtures to keep your clothes fresh, uncreased and dust-free, whether or not they are permanently on view.

Now for organization. Hang your evening clothes at one end of your cupboard bagged up in polythene for protection. Make sure the bags aren't too tight, or they will themselves cause creases. Follow on with your daytime clothes – hanging them in colour stories is often an aid to speedy dressing, as is a logical progression through dresses, skirts, trousers, blouses, jackets, rather than a random selection. That way short or flimsy items won't get concealed by more voluminous and bulky gear. Always leave as much space as possible in between garments – a layer of air allows them to breathe and prevents them getting squashed or creased. Position heavy coats, jackets and macs together at the opposite end of the rail from the evening wear.

Don't keep leather, fur or suede stored in polythene bags as skins sweat if enclosed in plastic and you run the risk of mould. Instead use a fabric bag or simple sheet cover that protects the skin and separates it from other clothing but allows some circulation of air.

If you have the space, hang shirts and blouses rather than fold them away in drawers, but be careful about hanging any

knitted wool or jersey knit dresses. If the hanger is well padded and the dress is light, close weave you may avoid sagging and stretching, but heavy or loosely knitted garments will lose their shape.

For the appearance of all your clothes it's worth investing in good coat-hangers; remember to top up your stock as you acquire new clothes. Plastic, wood or padded hangers are fine, but wire ones are to be avoided.

When you put a garment on its hanger, do up the buttons or zip so the item keeps its proper shape. Settle a collar, tie and sash, frill or flounce in position, hanging correctly and well supported by the weight of the whole item. Position shoulder seams along the line of the hanger if possible, so the extra strength of the seam takes the weight of the downward pull. Make sure the tips of the hangers are not pushing out a bump in the fabric on shoulders or sleeves. Padded

hangers are ideal for sensitive items. Some of the plastic types have sensibly sloped and rounded ends that allow a dress or blouse to fall smoothly from the shoulders. For skirts or trousers use clip-on or expandable hangers and let the waistband provide support for the correct hang of the clothing.

Divide up drawers or shelving so there is a specific area for each different type of clothes — undies and tights in one, sweaters in another and so on. Never over-fill drawers

otherwise, as with an over-stuffed wardrobe, your carefully pressed clothes will acquire creases before their next outing.

It's a good idea to line drawers to prevent delicate items getting snagged. Do up fastenings so they don't create an extra hazard. Save tights from incidental damage by keeping the plastic bags used in their packaging and return each pair of tights to an individual bag when they go back into the drawer after washing.

LIFESTYLES FASHIONSTYLES

Organize accessories so they are readily seen and selected. Belts are best hung by their buckles from a hook – never roll or fold them. Keep scarves folded in a visible stack so you can be reminded what's there and be inspired to use them with different outfits. If your jewellery collection is large, don't cram it all into one jewellery box; itemize earrings, necklaces, bangles or brooches into different boxes so you can see the possibilities at a glance.

You can enjoy working out not only the best way of assembling your accessories, but also the most attractive. A compartmented box, set of matching boxes or baskets, or a miniature chest of drawers can all be just as decorative as they are functional. If you like to keep everything concealed, belts can be hung from hooks fixed inside your cupboard doors but if you prefer to see what's on offer, you can hang them from an elegant wall-mounted coat rack or even a slimline, free-standing coat stand. The same goes for beads, chains and chunky jewellery, or if you have a large range of colourful, not-too-precious items, a simple kitchen mug-tree is an attractive and useful organizer.

Keep hats in shape and well protected. Stuff the crowns with paper and cover up with polythene, then store them in hat boxes or on a high shelf where there's no danger of something being inadvertently placed on top. Handbags, too, can be stuffed with tissue or newspaper to stay in shape.

Give your shoes reasonable space and don't let them get jumbled one on another. A shoe-rack is a relatively inexpensive investment that gives you additional vertical storage space. Otherwise range shoes in rows on the floor of your clothes cupboard or in an alcove and don't put away any that are muddy or wet when you take them off – follow the appropriate routine for cleaning and drying them. Use shoe-trees to maintain shoe-shape, or improvise by stuffing toes and heels with paper.

PACKING

There is only one way to make sure that you remember to pack all the items you need for a trip – make a list. Do it well in advance while there is still time to make additions and never put anything in the suitcase before you have checked it off on that list. Don't throw the list away – keep it to use as a starting point the next time your suitcases are brought out.

Traditional packers suggest starting with the heavy, bulky things like shoes – but that usually results in a bottom layer that imprints itself on your clothes. For an almost creaseless wardrobe at the end of your journey, try laying items like skirts or trousers dead flat at the bottom of the case. Build up with sweaters and jackets, leaving shoes and other odd-shaped items such as your wash-bag till last. If the first-in garments have been carefully folded this heavy top layer will act rather like a press. Stuff soft items like socks, tights and undies into the gaps. You can also put stray small objects inside shoes and pack these around the side of the case.

It is also a tradition of packing to use tissue paper to pad sleeves and separate layers of clothing. If you have the time, the patience and the tissue, there is no doubt that this works wonders.

When faced with creases on arrival, try hanging the offending article in the bathroom while you run a hot and steamy bath with the door shut. The creases should drop out. Unless you know exactly what you'll find at your destination, it's advisable to take some hangers with you in case the clothes closet is poorly equipped. If you don't have a travel iron, try using a hair-drier to blow-dry the creases away.

WASHING AND CLEANING

Always follow exactly the washing and cleaning instructions on the care labels inside your clothes. The hieroglyphics used to denote different courses of action are explained in the table below. If the label says 'dry clean' do follow that advice, however great the temptation to ignore it.

If it is possible to wet wash a garment take care to use water at the right temperature, whether the washing method is by hand or machine. Sort clothes according to the water temperature required for the fabric, at the same time separating articles of different colours. You can soak stubborn dirt before you wash if necessary, using a pre-wash soaking agent or your usual brand of washing powder. As with all cleaning agents, follow the brand product instructions printed on the packaging. The use of fabric softener in the final rinse is really a matter of personal preference. They are designed to leave fabrics soft and springy and help prevent matting of fibres, with the extra advantage that they do somewhat reduce the fabric's tendency to attract surface dirt.

If you have something which has lost its label and you can't absolutely identify the fibres, try to assess whether it is a fabric that should be dry cleaned. If not, hand wash it carefully in warm, not hot, water and don't subject it to the tumble drier. It may turn out to be quite robust but it's better to proceed with caution.

Always wash highly coloured items separately and don't leave clothes to soak if they are not colour fast, unless you are deliberately trying to create a faded effect. To test for colour fastness, damp a small area of the garment and press it with a warm iron between pieces of white cotton fabric. A non-fast colour should leave traces on the white fabric, but play safe anyway by keeping bright or strong colours separate from pastels and whites. Whether you air-dry or tumble-dry brightly coloured clothes, while they are still damp don't allow them to touch other items which may be marked by the colour.

Treat wool with special care, machine washing only if the label specifically approves that as a cleaning method. When hand washing wool, don't rub the fibres, rinse out thoroughly and always allow the clothing to dry flat – never tumble-dry wool. To remove excess moisture gently, roll up the garment in a folded towel and lightly squeeze the roll rather than wring it out. This treatment is useful for any fabric likely to suffer from spin drying, which sometimes seems to 'set' creases into the clothes.

To underline the words of caution about using a tumble drier, colours do seem to run here as easily as in the washing machine and the shrinkage of natural fabrics can be alarming. A drier is useful when you want a quick wash-and-wear job, however, so follow the label instructions and if in doubt about the effect of heat on a fabric, play safe and let it hang to dry naturally.

If your clothes need alterations or repairs, do these before washing or dry cleaning. When washing a summer-weight dress with shoulder pads you may find it more convenient to remove the pads first; mark their positions with a tacking thread so they are easily put back in place afterwards.

Check frequently to see which of your clothes would benefit from a trip to the dry cleaners and always have leather, suede or fur dealt with by the experts. Special evening clothes with a glittery or metallic surface effect can be brushed with a soft brush to remove surface dust and grime. A heavy winter coat or jacket for dry-cleaning only can be kept in condition by regular brushing and fluff removal. If you battle your way through polluted city air or get stuck in a cigarette-smoky atmosphere on the bus or train, it's a good idea to let your coat hang outside the clothes cupboard for a while, in the open air if possible to lose any staleness before it's put away among other clothing.

IRONING

A proper ironing board is an essential and an additional sleeve-board very useful. A plant water-spray for damping fabrics and a clean pressing cloth are invaluable accessories. The cloth may be a length of white muslin or thin cotton, or a drying-up cloth which is absorbent and resilient – but make sure it contains no colour that can come off on your clothes.

Follow label instructions and the temperature gauge on the iron to achieve the right heat for pressing different fabrics. If you are uncertain about a suitable temperature test the iron heat on the inside of a hem. Delicate fabrics likely to mark can be ironed under cloth or tissue. Start ironing at the section of the garment furthest away from you and work your way back so you don't have to fold or risk creasing a section you've already ironed. Press the wrong side (inside) of fabrics that are likely to become 'shiny' and always press seams and double layers, such as facings and hems, on the inside. Never wear clothes immediately after ironing, as they will instantly acquire new creases.

ON THE SPOT CLEANING

If you have the misfortune to stain, drop or spill something undesirable on your clothes, act very quickly. Don't leave it or you may find it's a permanent fixture. Washable clothes go straight into lukewarm water – too hot a tub may set the stain. For non-washable clothes the remedies are as broad and as various as the range of fabrics it is possible to be caught wearing.

As a guideline, if the stain is a greasy one, soak up as much as you can with talcum powder, deeply coloured liquid stains like wine or fruit should first be sprinkled with salt to absorb the colour; all other marks can be rubbed gently with a damp sponge – don't flood the stain or you may end up with a watermark as well. Whip the stained item smartly off to the dry cleaner and let them deal with the dirt that has been absorbed.

SHOES AND ACCESSORIES

Frequent cleaning, as we well know, prolongs the smart life of shoes. It's worth using one of the branded barrier creams to protect against water damage to new shoes. Never speed-dry wet leather shoes in direct heat; pack them with newspapers and dry slowly in a warm room. Make sure the leather has dried out completely before you apply shoe cream or polish. Remove caked mud with a stiff brush, dust with softer bristles. Dust off canvas shoes after each wearing to prevent grime becoming worked into the fabric.

Turn your handbags out regularly to throw away torn tissues or accumulated fluff that settles into the folds of the lining. Clean the outside of the bag as appropriate to the material, but be sparing with shoe cream or leather cleaner used to give your handbag a facelift. Buff it well with a soft cloth to remove any traces of colour that could rub off on your clothes next time you use the bag. Don't neglect any of your accessories – scarves, hats, gloves, and belts. They are supposed to enhance your outfit so they should be as clean and smart as the rest of your clothing.

 The garment can be hand- or machine-washed

 Do not wash

 The garment can be tumble-dried

 Do not tumble-dry

 The garment can be dry-cleaned in all solvents

 Do not dry-clean

 Hand-wash only

 The number below indicates the correct machine temperature

 The garment can be dried on a line

 The garment can be drip-dried

 Can be dry-cleaned in perchloroethylene, white spirit, solvents 111 and 113

 The fabric is sensitive and procedure Ⓟ must be modified

 Bleach may be used

 Do not use bleach

 The garment must be dried flat

 Do not iron

 The garment can be dry-cleaned in white spirit and solvent 113

 The fabric is sensitive and procedure Ⓕ must be modified

ACKNOWLEDGMENTS

■ PAGE 13: (Top) Black leather bodysuit, Azzedine Alaïa; Jewellery, Corocraft ■ PAGE 13: (Centre) Paisley blouse and tweed jacket, Ralph Lauren; Skirt, Stephen Marks; Lace handkerchief, Lunn Antiques; Boots, Hobbs; Gloves, Kir; Pearl brooch, Esther DeDeo at Ralph Lauren; Windsor chair, Crane Folk Art and Americana, 171a Sloane Street, SW1 ■ PAGE 13: (Bottom) Navy silk jersey dress and turquoise suede jacket, Jean Muir; Earrings, Butler and Wilson; Shoes and bag, Maud Frizon ■ PAGES 18-19: Satin shirts, Escada ■ PAGE 20: All clothes, Escada ■ PAGE 22: All clothes, Penny Black ■ PAGE 25: All clothes, Escada ■ PAGE 27: All clothes, Penny Black ■ PAGES 28-29: Leotards, Marks and Spencer ■ PAGE 35: Clothes, Laurel; Hat, Herbert Johnson ■ PAGES 36-37: All clothes, Kenzo ■ PAGES 38-39: Bandeau top, Sally Mee; White lawn shirt and cotton jersey leggings, Principles ■ PAGES 40-41: Coat, Stephen Marks; Shirt, Andrea Diamond; Trousers, Max Mara; Scarf, Souleiado; Satin jacket and skirt, Andrea Diamond ■ PAGE 42: Main picture as PAGE 40; Inset: Red wool dress, Stephen Marks ■ PAGE 43: All clothes, Andrea Diamond; Jewellery, Pellini ■ PAGES 46-49: All clothes, Warehouse, Demob and Buzz; Bags, Mulberrry; Scarves, Scotch House ■ PAGES 50-53: All clothes, Prisma ■ PAGES 54-57: All clothes, Benetton, Fenn Wright & Manson, French Connection and Aquascutum ■ PAGES 58-61: All clothes, Max Mara,

Alexon; Briefcase, Gold Pfeil; Jewellery, Pellini, Ken Lane ■ PAGES 62-63: Padded shoulder vest, Harvey Nichols; All other underwear, Marks and Spencer ■ PAGE 64: Dressing gown and pyjamas, The Scotch House ■ PAGE 65: Towelling robe, Principles ■ PAGES 66-67: Dress, Lorcan Mullany; Man's dinner suit, Jaeger ■ PAGE 69: Suit, Lorcan Mullany; Hat, The Hat Shop; Pearls, Adrien Mann; Bouquet, Jane Packer ■ PAGES 70-71: Spotted dress, Tatters; Jewellery, Marks and Spencer; Pink dress, David Feilden; Jewellery, Folli Folli; White suit, The Chelsea Design Company; Brooch, Pellini; Blue and black dress, Jacques Azagury; Earrings, Ken Lane ■ PAGE 72: Spotted dress, Caroline Charles; Necklace, Ken Lane ■ PAGE 73: Clothes, Lorcan Mullany; Jewellery, Pellini and Ken Lane ■ PAGES 74-75: Bikini, Lisa Bruce; Silk print separates, Sally Mee; Shorts, Principles ■ PAGE 76-77: All clothes, Marks and Spencer ■ PAGE 79: Aran sweater, Marks and Spencer; Mac, Mulberry; Breeches, Holland and Holland; Hat, The Hat Shop; Men's clothes, Holland and Holland ■ PAGE 80: Check suit, Stephen Marks; Silk shirt, Fenn Wright & Manson ■ PAGE 84: Shirt and cardigan, Solo ■ PAGE 87: Shirt, Principles; Scarf and pin, The Scotch House ■ PAGE 88: Jacket, Liz Claibourne; Sweater, Marks and Spencer ■ PAGE 91: Jacket, Stephen Marks ■ PAGE 94: Dress, Georges Rech; Belt, Nancy Fisher; Chair, Sheridan Coakley ■ PAGE 97: Coat, Cerrutti; Sweater, The Scotch House; Trousers, Sheridan Barnett; Belt, Mulberry; Hat, Fred Bare; Gloves, Dents; Shoes, Pied à Terre ■ PAGE 98: Suit,

Cerrutti; sweater, Fenn Wright & Manson; Bag, Mulberry; Spectacles, Emmanuelle Kahn ■ PAGE 100: Dress, Jacques Azagury; Earrings, Butler and Wilson ■ PAGE 101: Purple silk shirt and black crêpe skirt, Jasper Conran; Shoes, Pancaldi; Necklace, Eric Beamon ■ PAGE 102: Knitted jacket, Marion Foale; Silk blouse, Planet; Desk lamp and Canon typewriter, Joseph pour la Maison ■ PAGES 104-5: Blouse and skirt, Ungaro; Silver fox coat and hat, Bierger Christensen; Tights, Harvey Nichols; Jewellery, Butler and Wilson; Shoes, Maud Frizon ■ PAGE 106: Suit, Louis Féraud; Gloves, Cornelia James; Bag, Ungaro; Jewellery, Butler and Wilson; Shoes, Maud Frizon ■ PAGE 109: Coat and hat, Bierger Christensen ■ PAGE 110: Sweater, trousers and belt, Refine; Jewellery, Butler and Wilson ■ PAGE 111: Evening dress, Murrey Arbeid; Jewellery, Butler and Wilson; Gloves, Cornelia James ■ PAGE 112: shoes, Maud Frizon; Tights, Hanes ■ PAGE 114: Shirt and skirt, Viyella; Fair Isle waistcoat, Ralph Lauren; Cravat, fabric by Laura Ashley; Antique pin, Esther deDeo ■ PAGE 115: as PAGE 13, centre pic ■ PAGE 116: Embroidered satin waistcoat and silk blouse, Lunn Antiques; Skirt, Viyella; Gold watch chain, Theo Fennell; Cameo brooch, Imaginca ■ PAGE 117: Green pinafore, Laura Ashley; Linen

and lace blouse, Ralph Lauren; Velvet beret, Marida; Earrings, Michaela Frey ■ PAGE 119: Hand-embroidered calico smock, Julian Akers-Douglas; Brooch, Moss Bros ■ PAGE 120: Cotton Fair Isle jumper, Edina Ronay; Frilled shirt, Lunn Antiques; Scarf, Army and Navy Stores; Earrings, Michaela Frey ■ PAGE 121: Sheepskin jacket and flared skirt, Ally Capellino; Shirt, Tatters; Bow tie, Eximious; Gloves, Kir ■ PAGE 122: Bowler with pin, The Hat Shop; Veiling, Harrods; Blouse and waistcoat, Ralph Lauren; Brooch, Michaela Frey; Earrings, Imaginca ■ PAGE 123: Cream tights, Wolford; Lace-up boots, Russell and Bromley ■ PAGES 124-5: White blouson, striped bandeau and leggings, Buzz; Visor, The Hat Shop; Shoes, Palladium ■ PAGE 127: Jacket, skirt and shirt, Penny Black; Cap, The Hat Shop; Shoes, Palladium ■ PAGES 128-9: Matelot sweater and white trousers, Daniel Hechter; Cap, The Hat Shop ■ PAGE 131: Shirt, Lacoste; Shorts, Penny Black; Jersey, Laura Ashley ■ PAGE 132: Swimsuit, Speedo ■ PAGE 134: Gilet, John Partridge at Gordon Lowes; Skirt and shirt, Laura Ashley; Guernsey sweater, Force 4; Bag, Gucci; Pearls, Sloane Pearls; Scarf, Viyella ■ PAGES 136-7: Weatherproof coat, Barbour; Viyella shirt, Hilditch & Key; All other clothes from Gordon Lowes; Pearls, Sloane Pearls ■ PAGE 138: Balldress, Belville Sassoon; Pearl necklace, Sloane Pearls; Earrings, Michaela Frey ■ PAGE 139: Navy Loden coat and pleated skirt,

190

Gordon Lowes; Skirt, Hilditch & Key; Silk scarf, Hermès; Headband, Harrods; Tights, Wolford; Shoes, Gucci; Brooch, Jones ■ PAGE 140: Jewellery bugs, Jones ■ PAGE 141: Sweater, Warm and Wonderful; Scarf, Moss Bros; Bracelet, Michaela Frey ■ PAGE 143: Sweater, Martin Kidman; Rust ski pants, Miss Selfridge; Suede lace-ups, Johnny Moke ■ PAGE 145: Duffle coat and black trousers, Miss Selfridge; Shirt and polo-neck sweater, Marks and Spencer ■ PAGE 146: Black leather bodysuit, Azzedine Alaïa; Jewellery, Corocraft ■ PAGE 148: Yellow polo-neck and striped leggings, Miss Selfridge ■ PAGE 149: Cropped leather jacket and skirt, Pelle Studio; Striped T-Shirt, Rifat Ozbeck; Beret, Kangol ■ PAGE 150: Black bodyshirt, Jeff Banks; Tights, Harvey Nichols ■ PAGE 153: All clothes, Ralph Lauren; Shoes, Maud Frizon; Gloves Harrods ■ PAGE 155: Dress and jacket, Jean Muir; Earrings, Butler and Wilson; Shoes and bag, Maud Frizon ■ PAGE 156: Suit, blouse, belt and jewellery, Chanel ■ PAGE 157: Cotton sweaters, Marion Foale; Trousers, Ralph Lauren; Handbag, Mulberry; Earrings, Chanel ■ PAGE 158: Cashmere dressing gown, Browns; Silk pyjamas, Jean Muir ■ PAGE 163: Velvet swimsuit, Norma Kamali; White trousers, Jasper Conran; Earrings, Harvey Nichols; Black coolie hat, The Hat Shop ■ PAGE 164: Black top and skirt, Jasper Conran; Shoes, Charles Jourdan; Jewellery, Cobra & Bellamy ■ PAGE 167: Denim jacket, shorts and T-shirt, Michiko; Studded belt; Harvey Nichols; Sunglasses; Cutler and Gross ■ PAGES 168-9: All clothes, Jasper Conran; Hat, The Hat Shop ■ PAGE 171: Orange swimsuit and robe, Charles Jourdan;

Sunglasses, Cutler and Gross ■ PAGE 172: Australian army jacket, Lawrence Corner; Wrap-over crêpe skirt, American Classics; Hat, Hyper Hyper; Shoes, Katherine Hamnett; Jewellery, Pellini ■ PAGE 175: Skirt, American Classics; Frock coat, Miss Selfridge; Sleeveless polo top and flat pumps, Hobbs ■ PAGE 177: Raincoat and shirt, Blax; Trousers, American Classics; Shoes, Ad Hoc ■ PAGE 178: Pinstripe suit, Blax; Sweater, Help the Aged shop; Shoes, Ad Hoc ■ PAGE 179: Pinstripe trousers, Kensington Market; Boned waistcoat, Lunn Antiques; Shirt, Blax ■ PAGE 180: Black cocktail dress, American Classics; Hat, Portobello Road market; Gloves, Blax ■ PAGE 182: Silk nightdress, Lunn Antiques ■

PHOTOGRAPHY BY
■ JOHN BISHOP 13 bottom right, 16 centre, 50, 51, 53, 58, 60, 61, 94-95, 97, 98, 100, 101, 102, 152-3, 155, 156, 157, 158, 161

■ NICK BRIGGS 16 left, 16 right, 17 left and right, 28, 29, 30 bottom left, 30 bottom right, 34-35, 36-37, 38-9, 40, 41, 42, 43, 44, 45, 46, 47, 48, 49, 54, 55, 56, 62-3, 64, 65, 66-7, 69, 70-71, 72, 73, 74, 75, 76, 77, 79, 80, 81, 82-3, 84, 87, 88, 91, 134-5, 136, 137, 138, 139, 140, 141

■ SAM BROWN 13 top left, 142-3, 145, 146, 148, 149, 150, 172-3, 175, 177, 178, 179, 180, 182

■ RICHARD DUNKLEY 13 centre, 114, 115, 116, 117, 119, 120, 121, 122, 123, 128, 129, 131, 132

■ JAMES WEDGE 104-5, 106, 109, 110, 111, 112, 124-5, 127, 162-3, 164, 167, 168, 169, 171

■ VICTOR YUAN 18, 19, 20, 22, 25, 27, 30 top left, 30 top right

JACKET CREDITS
■ Front: Photographs by JOHN BISHOP (top left), JAMES WEDGE (top and bottom right) and RICHARD DUNKLEY (bottom left) ■ Back: Photographs by NICK BRIGGS (top) and JOHN BISHOP (bottom) ■ Front flap: Illustration by LYNNE ROBINSON ■ Back flap: Photograph by TONY McGEE

ILLUSTRATIONS BY
■ LYNNE ROBINSON

STYLING BY
■ KATHRYN SAMUEL, assisted by DEBBIE BEE, DEBBIE PAGE and KIM DOWNING

ADDITIONAL STYLING BY
■ JUDITH EAGLE (*New Beatnik*, pages 142-151)

■ ANNABEL HODIN (*Dynasty*, pages 104-113 and *Classic*, pages 152-161)

■ KIM HUNT (*Second-hand Rose*, pages 172-183)

■ CHRISTINE KNOX (*Country*, pages 114-123 and *Sloane*, pages 134-141)

■ The author and publishers would like to thank St Clement Danes Church, Strand, The Ritz, Piccadilly, and the Waldorf Hotel, Aldwych, for allowing us to photograph their premises

■ Pages 8-9 Oliviero Toscani/ Valentino; ■ 10 Rex Features Limited (left), Chanel (right); ■ 12 Niall McInerney; ■ 14 London Features International Limited/Neal Preston (left), Tim Graham (right); ■ 15 Frank Spooner Pictures/Gamma (top), Rex Features Limited (bottom).

■ The text for *Classic*, *Country* and *Dynasty* was written by SARAH LITVINOFF; for *New Beatnik* by JUDITH EAGLE; *Second-hand Rose* by KIM HUNT; and *Looking after your Clothes* by JUDY MARTIN.

LIFESTYLES FASHIONSTYLES